RANCH LIFE

AND

THE HUNTING-TRAIL

THE ROUND-UP.

RANCH LIFE

AND

THE HUNTING-TRAIL

BY

THEODORE ROOSEVELT

AUTHOR OF "HUNTING TRIPS OF A RANCHMAN,"
PRESIDENT OF THE BOONE AND CROCKETT CLUB OF NEW-YORK,
HONORARY MEMBER OF THE LONDON ALPINE CLUB, ETC., ETC.

ILLUSTRATED BY

FREDERIC REMINGTON

University of Nebraska Press
Lincoln and London

Manufactured in the United States of America.

First Bison Book printing: April 1983

Most recent printing indicated by the first digit below:
4   5   6   7   8   9   10

Library of Congress Cataloging in Publication Data
Roosevelt, Theodore, 1858–1919.
  Ranch life and the hunting-trail.

  Reprint. Previously published: New York : Century,
1901.
  1. Ranch life—West (U.S.) 2. Cowboys—West (U.S.)
3. Hunting—West (U.S.) 4. Ranch life—North Dakota.
5. Cowboys—North Dakota. 6. Hunting—North Dakota.
7. West (U.S.)—Description and travel—1880–1950.
8. Roosevelt, Theodore, 1858–1919—Homes—North Dakota.
I. Remington, Frederic, 1861–1909. II. Title
[F596.R78 1983]   978   82-20091
ISBN 0-8032-3865-7
ISBN 0-8032-8913-8 (pbk.)

∞

Reprinted from the first edition, published in 1888.

TABLE OF CONTENTS

"Oh, our manhood's prime vigor ! No spirit feels waste,
Not a muscle is stopped in its playing nor sinew unbraced.
Oh, the wild joys of living ! the leaping from rock up to rock,
The strong rending of boughs from the fir-tree, the cool silver shock
Of the plunge in a pool's living water, the hunt of the bear, . . .
And the sleep in the dried river-channel where bulrushes tell
That the water was wont to go warbling so softly and well.
How good is man's life, the mere living."

BROWNING.

RANCH LIFE AND THE HUNTING-TRAIL

A STUDY FROM LIFE.

Ranch Life and the Hunting-Trail

I

The Cattle Country of the Far West

THE great grazing lands of the West lie in what is known as the arid belt, which stretches from British America on the north to Mexico on the south, through the middle of the United States. It includes New Mexico, part of Arizona, Colorado, Wyoming, Montana, and the western portion of Texas, Kansas, Nebraska, and Dakota. It must not be understood by this that more cattle are to be found here than elsewhere, for the contrary is true, it being a fact often lost sight of that the number of cattle raised on the small, thick-lying farms of the fertile Eastern States is actually many times greater than that of those scattered over the vast, barren ranches of the far West; for stock will always be most plentiful in districts where corn and other winter food can be grown. But in this arid belt, and in this arid belt only,—save in a few similar tracts on the Pacific slope,—stock-raising is almost the sole industry, except in the mountain districts where there is mining. The whole region is one vast stretch of grazing country, with only here and there spots of farm-land, in most places there being nothing more like agriculture than is implied in the cutting of some tons of wild hay or the planting of a garden patch for home use. This is especially true of the northern portion of the region, which comprises the basin of the Upper Missouri, and with which alone I am familiar. Here there are no fences to speak of, and all the land north of the Black Hills and the Big Horn Mountains and between the Rockies and the Dakota wheat-fields might be spoken of as one gigantic, unbroken pasture, where cowboys and branding-irons take the place of fences.

The country throughout this great Upper Missouri basin has a wonderful sameness of character; and the rest of the arid belt, lying to the southward, is closely akin to it in its main features. A traveler seeing it for the first time is especially struck by its look of parched, barren desolation; he can with difficulty believe that it will support cattle at all. It is a region of light rainfall; the grass is short and comparatively scanty; there is no timber except along the beds of the streams, and in many places there are alkali deserts where nothing grows but sage-brush and cactus. Now the land stretches out into level, seemingly endless plains or into rolling prairies; again it is broken by abrupt hills and deep, winding valleys; or else it is crossed by chains of buttes, usually bare, but often clad with a dense growth of dwarfed pines or gnarled, stunted cedars. The muddy rivers run in broad, shallow beds, which after heavy rainfalls are filled to the brim by the swollen torrents, while in droughts the larger streams dwindle into sluggish trickles of clearer water, and the smaller ones dry up entirely, save in occasional deep pools.

All through the region, except on the great Indian reservations, there has been a scanty and sparse settlement, quite peculiar in its character. In the forest the woodchopper comes first; on the fertile prairies the granger is the pioneer; but on the long, stretching uplands of the far West it is the men who guard and follow the horned herds that prepare the way for the settlers who come after. The high plains of the Upper Missouri and its tributary rivers were first opened, and are still held, by the stockmen, and the whole civilization of the region has received the stamp of their marked and individual characteristics. They were from the South, not from the East, although many men from the latter region came out along the great transcontinental railway lines and joined them in their northern migration.

They were not dwellers in towns, and from the nature of their industry lived as far apart from each other as possible. In choosing new ranges, old cow-hands, who are also seasoned plainsmen, are invariably sent ahead, perhaps a year in advance, to spy out the land and pick the best places. One of these may go by himself, or more often, especially if they have to penetrate little known or entirely unknown tracts, two or three will go together, the owner or manager of the herd himself being one of them. Perhaps their herds may already be on the border of the wild and uninhabited country: in that case they may have to take but a few days' journey before finding the stretches of sheltered, long-grass land that they seek. For instance, when I wished to move my own elkhorn steer brand on to a new ranch I had to spend barely a week in traveling north among the Little Missouri Bad Lands before finding what was then untrodden ground far outside the range of any of my neighbors' cattle. But if a large outfit is going to shift its quarters it must go much farther; and both

AN EXPLORING OUTFIT.

the necessity and the chance for long wanderings were especially great when the final overthrow of the northern Horse Indians opened the whole Upper Missouri basin at one sweep to the stockmen. Then the advance-guards or explorers, each on one horse and leading another with food and bedding, were often absent months at a time, threading their way through the trackless wastes of plain, plateau, and river-bottom. If possible they would choose a country that would be good for winter and summer alike; but often this could not be done, and then they would try to find a well-watered tract on which the cattle could be summered, and from which they could be driven in fall to their sheltered winter range—for the cattle in winter eat snow, and an entirely waterless region, if broken, and with good pasturage, is often the best possible winter ground, as it is sure not to have been eaten off at all during the summer; while in the bottoms the grass is always cropped down soonest. Many outfits regularly shift their herds every spring and fall; but with us in the Bad Lands all we do, when cold weather sets in, is to drive our beasts off the scantily grassed river-bottom back ten miles or more among the broken buttes and plateaus of the uplands to where the brown hay, cured on the stalk, stands thick in the winding coulees.

These lookouts or forerunners having returned, the herds are set in motion as early in the spring as may be, so as to get on the ground in time to let the travel-worn beasts rest and gain flesh before winter sets in. Each herd is accompanied by a dozen, or a score, or a couple of score, of cowboys, according to its size, and beside it rumble and jolt the heavy four-horse wagons that hold the food and bedding of the men and the few implements they will need at the end of their journey. As long as possible they follow the trails made by the herds that have already traveled in the same direction, and when these end they strike out for themselves. In the Upper Missouri basin, the pioneer herds soon had to scatter out and each find its own way among the great dreary solitudes, creeping carefully along so that the cattle should not be overdriven and should have water at the halting-places. An outfit might thus be months on its lonely journey, slowly making its way over melancholy, pathless plains, or down the valleys of the lonely rivers. It was tedious, harassing work, as the weary cattle had to be driven carefully and quietly during the day and strictly guarded at night, with a perpetual watch kept for Indians or white horse-thieves. Often they would skirt the edges of the streams for days at a time, seeking for a ford or a good swimming crossing, and if the water was up and the quicksand deep the danger to the riders was serious and the risk of loss among the cattle very great.

At last, after days of excitement and danger and after months of weary, monotonous toil, the chosen ground is reached and the final camp pitched. The footsore animals are turned loose to shift for themselves, outlying camps of two or three men each being established to hem them in. Meanwhile the primitive ranch-house, out-buildings, and corrals are built, the unhewn cottonwood logs being chinked with moss and mud, while the roofs are of branches covered with dirt, spades and axes being the only tools needed for the work. Bunks, chairs, and tables are all home-made, and as rough as the houses they are in. The supplies of coarse, rude food

THE MIDDAY MEAL.

are carried perhaps two or three hundred miles from the nearest town, either in the ranch-wagons or else by some regular freighting outfit, the huge canvas-topped prairie schooners of which are each drawn by several yoke of oxen, or perhaps by six or eight mules. To guard against the numerous mishaps of prairie travel, two or three of these prairie schooners usually go together, the brawny teamsters, known either as "bull-whack-ers" or as "mule-skinners," stalking beside their slow-moving teams.

The small outlying camps are often tents, or mere dug-outs in the ground. But at the main ranch there will be a cluster of log buildings, including a separate cabin for the foreman or ranchman; often another in which to cook and eat; a long house for the men to sleep in; stables, sheds, a blacksmith's shop, etc.,—the whole group forming quite a little settlement, with the corrals, the stacks of natural hay, and the patches of fenced land for gardens or horse pastures. This little settlement may be situated right out in the treeless, nearly level open, but much more often is placed in the partly wooded bottom of a creek or river, sheltered by the usual background of somber brown hills.

3

When the northern plains began to be settled, such a ranch would at first be absolutely alone in the wilderness, but others of the same sort were sure soon to be established within twenty or thirty miles on one side or the other. The lives of the men in such places were strangely cut off from the outside world, and, indeed, the same is true to a hardly less extent at the present day. Sometimes the wagons are sent for provisions, and the beef-steers are at stated times driven off for shipment. Parties of hunters and trappers call now and then. More rarely small bands of emigrants go by in search of new homes, impelled by the restless, aimless craving for change so deeply grafted in the breast of the American borderer: the white-topped wagons are loaded with domestic goods, with sallow, dispirited-looking women, and with tow-headed children; while the gaunt, moody frontiersmen slouch alongside, rifle on shoulder, lank, homely, uncouth, and yet with a curious suggestion of grim strength underlying it all. Or cowboys from neighboring ranches will ride over, looking for lost horses, or seeing if their cattle have strayed off the range. But this is all. Civilization seems as remote as if we were living in an age long past. The whole existence is patriarchal in character: it is the life of men who live in the open, who tend their herds on horseback, who go armed and ready to guard their lives by their own prowess, whose wants are very simple, and who call no man master. Ranching is an occupation like those of vigorous, primitive pastoral peoples, having little in common with the humdrum, workaday business world of the nineteenth century; and the free ranchman in his manner of life shows more kinship to an Arab sheik than to a sleek city merchant or tradesman.

By degrees the country becomes what in a stock-raising region passes for well settled. In addition to the great ranches smaller ones are established, with a few hundred, or even a few score, head of cattle apiece; and now and then miserable farmers straggle in to fight a losing and desperate battle with drought, cold, and grasshoppers. The wheels of the heavy wagons, driven always over the same course from one ranch to another, or to the remote frontier towns from which they get their goods, wear ruts in the soil, and roads are soon formed, perhaps originally following the deep trails made by the vanished buffalo. These roads lead down the river-bottoms or along the crests of the divides or else strike out fairly across the prairie, and a man may sometimes journey a hundred miles along one without coming to a house or a camp of any sort. If they lead to a shipping point whence the beeves are sent to market, the cattle, traveling in single file, will have worn many and deep paths on each side of the wheel-marks; and the roads between important places which are regularly used either by the United States Government, by stage-coach lines, or by freight teams become deeply worn landmarks—as, for instance, near us, the Deadwood and the old Fort Keogh trails.

Cattle-ranching can only be carried on in its present form while the population is scanty; and so in stock-raising regions, pure and simple, there are usually few towns, and these are almost always at the shipping points for cattle. But, on the other hand, wealthy cattlemen, like miners who have done well, always spend their money freely; and accordingly towns like Denver, Cheyenne, and Helena, where these two classes are the most influential in the community, are far pleasanter places of residence than cities of five times their population in the exclusively agricultural States to the eastward.

A true "cow town" is worth seeing,—such a one as Miles City, for instance, especially at the time of the annual meeting of the great Montana Stock-raisers' Association. Then the whole place is full to overflowing, the importance of the meeting and the fun of the attendant frolics, especially the horse-races, drawing from the surrounding ranch country many hundreds of men of every degree, from the rich stock-owner worth his millions to the ordinary cowboy who works for forty dollars a month. It would be impossible to imagine a more typically American assemblage, for although there are always a certain number of foreigners, usually English, Irish, or German, yet they have become completely Americanized; and on the whole it would be difficult to gather a finer body of men, in spite of their numerous shortcomings. The ranch-owners differ more from each other than do the cowboys; and the former certainly compare very favorably with similar classes of capitalists in the East. Anything more foolish than the demagogic outcry against "cattle kings" it would be difficult to imagine. Indeed, there are very few businesses so absolutely legitimate as stock-raising and so beneficial to the nation at large; and a successful stock-grower must not only be shrewd, thrifty, patient, and enterprising, but he must also possess qualities of personal bravery, hardihood, and self-reliance to a degree not demanded in the least by any mercantile occupation in a community long settled. Stockmen are in the West the pioneers of civilization, and their daring and adventurousness make the after settlement of the region possible. The whole country owes them a great debt.

The most successful ranchmen are those, usually South-westerners, who have been bred to the business and have grown up with it; but many Eastern men, including not a few college graduates, have also done excellently by devoting their whole time and energy to their work,—

although Easterners who invest their money in cattle without knowing anything of the business, or who trust all to their subordinates, are naturally enough likely to incur heavy losses.   Stockmen are learning more

THE OUTLYING CAMP.

and more to act together; and certainly the meetings of their associations are conducted with a dignity and good sense that would do credit to any parliamentary body.

But the cowboys resemble one another much more and outsiders much less than is the case even with their employers, the ranchmen.   A town in the cattle country, when for some cause it is thronged with men from the neighborhood, always presents a picturesque sight.   On the wooden sidewalks of the broad, dusty streets the men who ply the various industries known only to frontier existence jostle one another as they saunter to and fro or lounge lazily in front of the straggling, cheap-looking board houses.   Hunters come in from the plains and the mountains, clad in buckskin shirts and fur caps, greasy and unkempt, but with resolute faces and sullen, watchful eyes, that are ever on the alert.   The teamsters, surly and self-contained, wear slouch hats and great cowhide boots; while the stage-drivers, their faces seamed by the hardship and exposure of their long drives with every kind of team, through every kind of country, and in every kind of weather, proud of their really wonderful skill as reinsmen and conscious of their high standing in any frontier community, look down on and sneer at the "skin hunters" and the plodding drivers of the white-topped prairie schooners. Besides these there are trappers, and wolfers, whose business is to poison wolves, with shaggy, knock-kneed ponies to carry their small bales and bundles of furs — beaver, wolf, fox, and occasionally otter; and silent sheep-herders, with cast-down faces, never able to forget the absolute solitude and monotony of their dreary lives, nor to rid their minds of the thought of the woolly idiots they pass all their days in tending. Such are the men who have come to town, either on business or else to frequent the flaunting saloons and gaudy hells of all kinds in search of the coarse, vicious excitement that in the minds of many of them does duty as pleasure — the only form of pleasure they have ever had a chance to know. Indians too, wrapped in blankets, with stolid, emotionless faces, stalk silently round among the whites, or join in the gambling and horse-racing. If the town is on the borders of the mountain country, there will also be sinewy lumbermen, rough-looking miners, and packers, whose business it is to guide the long mule and pony trains that go where wagons can not and whose work in packing needs special and peculiar skill; and mingled with and drawn from all these classes are desperadoes of every grade, from the gambler up through the horse-thief to the murderous professional bully, or, as he is locally called, "bad man"— now, however, a much less conspicuous object than formerly.

But everywhere among these plainsmen and mountain-men, and more important than any, are the cowboys,— the men who follow the calling that has brought such towns into being. Singly, or in twos or threes, they gallop their wiry little horses down the street, their lithe, supple figures erect or swaying slightly as they sit loosely in the saddle; while their stirrups are so long that their knees are hardly bent, the bridles not taut enough to keep the chains from clanking. They are smaller and less muscular than the wielders of ax and pick; but they are as hardy and self-reliant as any men who ever breathed — with bronzed, set faces, and keen eyes that look all the world straight in the face without flinching as they flash out from under the broad-brimmed hats. Peril and hardship, and years of long toil broken by weeks of brutal dissipation, draw haggard lines across their eager faces, but never dim their reckless eyes nor break their bearing of defiant self-confidence. They do not walk well, partly because they so rarely do any work out of the saddle, partly because their *chaperajos* or leather overalls hamper them when on the ground; but their appearance is striking for all that, and picturesque too, with their jingling spurs, the big revolvers stuck in their belts, and bright silk handkerchiefs knotted loosely round their necks over the open collars of the flannel shirts.   When drunk on the villainous whisky of the frontier towns, they cut mad antics, riding their horses into the saloons, firing their pistols right and left, from boisterous light-heartedness rather than from any viciousness, and indulging too often in deadly shooting affrays, brought on either by the accidental contact of the moment or on account of some long-standing grudge, or perhaps because of bad blood between two ranches or localities; but except while on such sprees they are quiet, rather self-contained men, perfectly frank and simple, and on their own ground treat a stranger with the most whole-souled hospitality, doing all in their power for him and scorning to take any reward in return. Although prompt to resent an injury, they are not at all apt to be rude to outsiders, treating them with what can almost be called a grave court-esy.   They are much better fellows and pleasanter companions than small farmers or agricultural laborers; nor are the mechanics and workmen of a great city to be mentioned in the same breath.

The bulk of the cowboys themselves are South-westerners; but there are also many from the Eastern and the Northern States, who, if they begin young, do quite as well as the Southerners.   The best hands are fairly bred to the work and follow it from their youth up. Nothing can be more foolish than for an Easterner to think he can become a cowboy in a few months' time.   Many a young fellow comes out hot with enthusiasm for life on the plains, only to learn that his clumsiness is greater than he could have believed possible; that the cowboy business is like any other and has to be learned by serving a painful apprenticeship; and that this apprenticeship implies the endurance of rough fare, hard living, dirt, exposure of every kind, no little toil, and month after month of the dull-est monotony.   For cowboy work there is need of special traits and special training, and young Easterners should be sure of themselves before trying it: the struggle for existence is very keen in the far West, and it is no place for men who lack the ruder, coarser virtues and physical qualities, no matter how intellectual or how refined and delicate their sensibilities. Such are more likely to fail there than in older communities. Probably during the past few years more than half of the young Eastern-ers who have come West with a little money to learn the cattle business have failed signally and lost what they had in the beginning.   The West, especially the far West, needs men who have been bred on the farm or in the workshop far more than it does clerks or college graduates.

COWBOY FUN.

Some of the cowboys are Mexicans, who generally do the actual work well enough, but are not trustworthy; moreover, they are always regarded with extreme disfavor by the Texans in an outfit, among whom the intolerant caste spirit is very strong. Southern-born whites will never work under them, and look down upon all colored or half-caste races. One spring I had with my wagon a Pueblo Indian, an excellent rider and roper, but a drunken, worthless, lazy devil; and in the summer of 1886 there were with us a Sioux half-breed, a quiet, hard-working, faithful fellow, and a mulatto, who was one of the best cow-hands in the whole round-up.

Cowboys, like most Westerners, occasionally show remarkable versatility in their tastes and pursuits. One whom I know has abandoned his regular occupation for the past nine months, during which time he has been in succession a bartender, a school-teacher, and a probate judge! Another, whom I once employed for a short while, had passed through even more varied experiences, including those of a barber, a sailor, an apothecary, and a buffalo-hunter.

As a rule the cowboys are known to each other only by their first names, with, perhaps, as a prefix, the title of the brand for which they are working. Thus I remember once overhearing a casual remark to the effect that "Bar Y Harry" had married "the Seven Open A girl," the latter being the daughter of a neighboring ranchman. Often they receive

IN A BOG-HOLE.

nicknames, as, for instance, Dutch Wannigan, Windy Jack, and Kid Williams, all of whom are on the list of my personal acquaintances.

No man traveling through or living in the country need fear molestation from the cowboys unless he himself accompanies them on their drinking-bouts, or in other ways plays the fool, for they are, with us at any rate, very good fellows, and the most determined and effective foes of real law-breakers, such as horse and cattle thieves, murderers, etc. Few of the outrages quoted in Eastern papers as their handiwork are such in reality, the average Easterner apparently considering every individual who wears a broad hat and carries a six-shooter a cowboy. These outrages are, as a rule, the work of the roughs and criminals who always gather on the outskirts of civilization, and who infest every frontier town until the decent citizens become sufficiently numerous and determined to take the law into their own hands and drive them out. The old buffalo-hunters, who formed a distinct class, became powerful forces for evil once they had destroyed the vast herds of mighty beasts the pursuit of which had been their means of livelihood. They were absolutely shiftless and improvident; they had no settled habits; they were inured to peril and hardship, but entirely unaccustomed to steady work; and so they afforded just the materials from which to make the bolder and more desperate kinds of criminals. When the game was gone they hung round the settlements for some little time, and then many of them naturally took to horse-stealing, cattle-killing, and highway robbery, although others, of course, went into honest pursuits. They were men who died off rapidly, however; for it is curious to see how many of these plainsmen, in spite of their iron nerves and thews, have their constitutions completely undermined, as much by the terrible hardships they have endured as by the fits of prolonged and bestial revelry with which they have varied them.

The "bad men," or professional fighters and man-killers, are of a different stamp, quite a number of them being, according to their light, perfectly honest. These are the men who do most of the killing in frontier communities; yet it is a noteworthy fact that the men who are killed generally deserve their fate. These men are, of course, used to brawling, and are not only sure shots, but, what is equally important, able to "draw" their weapons with marvelous quickness. They think nothing whatever of murder, and are the dread and terror of their associates; yet they are very chary of taking the life of a man of good standing, and will often weaken and back down at once if confronted fearlessly. With many of them their courage arises from confidence in their own powers and knowledge of the fear in which they are held; and men of this type often show the white feather when they get in a tight place. Others, however, will face any odds without flinching; and I have known of these men fighting, when mortally wounded, with a cool, ferocious despair that was terrible. As elsewhere, so here, very quiet men are often those who in an emergency show themselves best able to hold their own. These desperadoes always try to "get the drop" on a foe—that is, to take him at a disadvantage before he can use his own weapon. I have known more

4

men killed in this way, when the affair was wholly one-sided, than I have known to be shot in fair fight; and I have known fully as many who were shot by accident. It is wonderful, in the event of a street fight, how few bullets seem to hit the men they are aimed at.

During the last two or three years the stockmen have united to put down all these dangerous characters, often by the most summary exercise of lynch law. Notorious bullies and murderers have been taken out and hung, while the bands of horse and cattle thieves have been regularly hunted down and destroyed in pitched fights by parties of armed cowboys; and as a consequence most of our territory is now perfectly law-abiding. One such fight occurred north of me early last spring. The horse-thieves were overtaken on the banks of the Missouri; two of their number were slain, and the others were driven on the ice, which broke, and two more were drowned. A few months previously another gang, whose headquarters were near the Canadian line, were surprised in their hut; two or three were shot down by the cowboys as they tried to come out, while the rest barricaded themselves in and fought until the great log-hut was set on fire, when they broke forth in a body, and nearly all were killed at once, only one or two making their escape. A little over two years ago one committee of vigilantes in eastern Montana shot or hung nearly sixty — not, however, with the best judgment in all cases.

OUT ON THE RANGE

THE BRANDING CHUTE.

II

OUT ON THE RANGE

A STRANGER in the North-western cattle country is especially struck by the resemblance the settlers show in their pursuits and habits to the Southern people. Nebraska and Dakota, east of the Missouri, resemble Minnesota and Iowa and the States farther east, but Montana and the Dakota cow country show more kinship with Texas; for while elsewhere in America settlement has advanced along the parallels of latitude, on the great plains it has followed the meridians of longitude and has gone northerly rather than westerly. The business is carried on as it is in the South. The rough-rider of the plains, the hero of rope and revolver, is first cousin to the backwoodsman of the southern Alleghanies, the man of the ax and the rifle; he is only a unique offshoot of the frontier stock of the South-west. The very term "round-up" is used by the cowboys in the exact sense in which it is employed by the hill people and mountaineers of Kentucky, Tennessee, and North Carolina, with whom also labor is dear and poor land cheap, and whose few cattle are consequently branded and turned loose in the woods exactly as is done with the great herds on the plains.

But the ranching industry itself was copied from the Mexicans, of whose land and herds the South-western frontiersmen of Texas took forcible possession; and the traveler in the North-west will see at a glance that the terms and practices of our business are largely of Spanish origin. The cruel curb-bit and heavy stock-saddle, with its high horn and cantle, prove that we have adopted Spanish-American horse-gear; and the broad hat, huge blunt spurs, and leather *chaperajos* of the rider, as well as the corral in which the stock are penned, all alike show the same ancestry. Throughout the cattle country east of the Rocky Mountains, from the Rio Grande to the Saskatchewan, the same terms are in use and the same system is followed; but on the Pacific slope, in California, there are certain small differences, even in nomenclature. Thus, we of the great plains all use the double cinch saddle, with one girth behind the horse's fore legs and another farther back, while Californians prefer one with a single cinch, which seems to us much inferior for stock-work. Again, Californians use the Spanish word "lasso," which with us has been entirely dropped, no plainsman with pretensions to the title thinking of any word but "rope," either as noun or verb.

The rope, whether leather lariat or made of grass, is the one essential feature of every cowboy's equipment. Loosely coiled, it hangs from the horn or is tied to one side of the saddle in front of the thigh, and is used for every conceivable emergency, a twist being taken round the stout saddle-horn the second the noose settles over the neck or around the legs of a chased animal. In helping pull a wagon up a steep pitch, in dragging an animal by the horns out of a bog-hole, in hauling logs for the fire, and in a hundred other ways aside from its legitimate purpose, the rope is of invaluable service, and dexterity with it is prized almost or quite as highly as good horsemanship, and is much rarer. Once a cowboy is a good roper and rider, the only other accomplishment he values is skill with his great army revolver, it being taken for granted that he is already a thorough plainsman and has long mastered the details of cattle-work; for the best roper and rider alive is of little use unless he is hard-working, honest, keenly alive to his employer's interest, and very careful in the management of the cattle.

All cowboys can handle the rope with more or less ease and precision, but great skill in its use is only attained after long practice, and for its highest development needs that the man should have begun in earliest youth. Mexicans literally practice from infancy; the boy can hardly toddle before he gets a string and begins to render life a burden to the hens, goats, and pigs. A really first-class roper can command his own price, and is usually fit for little but his own special work.

It is much the same with riding. The cowboy is an excellent rider in his own way, but his way differs from that of a trained school horseman or cross-country fox-hunter as much as it does from the horsemanship of an Arab or of a Sioux Indian, and, as with all these, it has its special merits and special defects—schoolman, fox-hunter, cowboy, Arab, and Indian being all alike admirable riders in their respective styles, and each cherishing the same profound and ignorant contempt for every method but his own. The flash riders, or horse-breakers, always called "bronco busters," can perform really marvelous feats, riding with ease the most vicious and unbroken beasts, that no ordinary cowboy would dare to tackle. Although sitting seemingly so loose in the saddle, such a rider cannot be jarred out of it by the wildest plunges, it being a favorite feat to sit out the antics of a bucking horse with silver half-dollars under each knee or in the stirrups under each foot. But their method of breaking is very rough, consist-

PULLING A COW OUT OF THE MUD.

ing only in saddling and bridling a beast by main force and then riding him, also by main force, until he is exhausted, when he is turned over as "broken." Later on the cowboy himself may train his horse to stop or wheel instantly at a touch of the reins or bit, to start at top speed at a signal, and to stand motionless when left. An intelligent pony soon picks up a good deal of knowledge about the cow business on his own account.

All cattle are branded, usually on the hip, shoulder, and side, or on any one of them, with letters, numbers, or figures, in every combination, the outfit being known by its brand. Near me, for instance, are the Three Sevens, the Thistle, the Bellows, the OX, the VI., the Seventy-six Bar ($\frac{76}{}$), and the Quarter Circle Diamond ($\diamondsuit$) outfits. The dew-lap and the ears may also be cut, notched, or slit. All brands are registered, and are thus protected against imitators, any man tampering with them being punished as severely as possible. Unbranded animals are called *mavericks,* and when found on the round-up are either branded by the owner of the range on which they are, or else are sold for the benefit of the association. At every shipping point, as well as where the beef cattle are received, there are stock inspectors who jealously examine all the brands on the live animals or on the hides of the slaughtered ones, so as to detect any foul play, which is immediately reported to the association. It becomes second nature with a cowboy to inspect and note the brands of every bunch of animals he comes across.

Perhaps the thing that seems strangest to the traveler who for the first time crosses the bleak plains of this Upper Missouri grazing country is the small number of cattle seen. He can hardly believe he is in the great stock region, where for miles upon miles he will not see a single head, and will then come only upon a straggling herd of a few score. As a matter of fact, where there is no artificial food put up for winter use cattle always need a good deal of ground per head; and this is peculiarly the case with us in the North-west, where much of the ground is bare of vegetation and where what pasture there is is both short and sparse. It is a matter of absolute necessity, where beasts are left to shift for themselves in the open during the bitter winter weather, that they then should have grass that they have not cropped too far down; and to insure this it is necessary with us to allow on the average about twenty-five acres of ground to each animal. This means that a range of country ten miles square will keep between two and three thousand head of stock only, and if more are put on, it is at the risk of seeing a severe winter kill off half or three-quarters of the whole number. So a range may be in reality overstocked when to an Eastern and unpracticed eye it seems hardly to have on it a number worth taking into account.

Overstocking is the great danger threatening the stock-raising industry on the plains. This industry has only risen to be of more than local consequence during the past score of years, as before that time it was confined to Texas and California; but during these two decades of its existence the stockmen in different localities have again and again suffered the most ruinous losses, usually with overstocking as the ultimate cause. In the south the drought, and in the north the deep snows, and everywhere unusually bad winters, do immense damage; still, if the land is fitted for stock at all, they will, averaging one year with another, do very well so long as the feed is not cropped down too close.

But, of course, no amount of feed will make some countries worth anything for cattle that are not housed during the winter; and stockmen in choosing new ranges for their herds pay almost as much attention to the capacity of the land for yielding shelter as they do to the abundant and good quality of the grass. High up among the foot-hills of the mountains cattle will not live through the winter; and an open, rolling prairie land of heavy rainfall, where in consequence the snow lies deep and there is no protection from the furious cold winds, is useless for winter grazing, no matter how thick and high the feed. The three essentials for a range are grass, water, and shelter: the water is only needed in summer and the shelter in winter, while it may be doubted if drought during the hot months has ever killed off more cattle than have died of exposure on shelterless ground to the icy weather, lasting from November to April.

The finest summer range may be valueless either on account of its lack of shelter or because it is in a region of heavy snowfall — portions of territory lying in the same latitude and not very far apart often differing widely in this respect, or extraordinarily severe weather may cause a heavy death-rate utterly unconnected with overstocking. This was true of the loss that visited the few herds which spent the very hard winter of 1880 on the northern cattle plains. These were the pioneers of their kind, and the grass was all that could be desired; yet the extraordinary severity of the weather proved too much for the cattle. This was especially the case with those herds consisting of "pilgrims," as they are called — that is, of animals driven up on to the range from the south, and therefore in poor condition. One such herd of pilgrims on the Powder River suffered a loss of thirty-six hundred out of a total of four thousand, and the survivors kept alive only by browsing on the tops of cottonwoods felled for them. Even seasoned animals fared very badly. One great herd in the Yellowstone Valley lost about a fourth of its number, the loss falling mainly on the breeding cows, calves, and bulls,— always the chief sufferers, as the steers, and also the dry cows, will get through almost anything. The loss here would have been far heavier than it was had it not been for a curious trait shown by the cattle. They kept in bands of several hundred each, and during the time of the deep snows a band would make a start and travel several miles in a straight line, plowing their way through the drifts and beating out a broad track; then, when stopped by a frozen water-course or chain of buttes, they would turn back and graze over the trail thus made, the only place where they could get at the grass.

A drenching rain, followed by a severe snap of cold, is even more destructive than deep snow, for the saturated coats of the poor beasts are turned into sheets of icy mail, and the grass-blades, frozen at the roots as well as above, change into sheaves of brittle spears as uneatable as so

5

many icicles. Entire herds have perished in consequence of such a storm. Mere cold, however, will kill only very weak animals, which is fortunate for us, as the spirit in the thermometer during winter often sinks to fifty degrees below zero, the cold being literally arctic; yet though the cattle become thin during such a snap of weather, and sometimes have their ears, tails, and even horns frozen off, they nevertheless rarely die from the cold alone.   But if there is a blizzard blowing at such a time, the cattle

A DISPUTE OVER A BRAND.

need shelter, and if caught in the open, will travel for scores of miles before the storm, until they reach a break in the ground, or some stretch of dense woodland, which will shield them from the blasts.   If cattle traveling in this manner come to some obstacle that they cannot pass, as, for instance, a wire fence or a steep railway embankment, they will not try to make their way back against the storm, but will simply stand with their tails to it until they drop dead in their tracks; and, accordingly, in some parts of the country — but luckily far to the south of us — the railways are fringed with countless skeletons of beasts that have thus perished, while many of the long wire fences make an almost equally bad showing.

In some of the very open country of Kansas and Indian Territory, many of the herds during the past two years have suffered a loss of from sixty to eighty per cent., although this was from a variety of causes, including drought as well as severe winter weather. Too much rain is quite as bad as too little, especially if it falls after the 1st of August, for then, though the growth of grass is very rank and luxuriant, it yet has little strength and does not cure well on the stalk; and it is only possible to winter cattle at large at all because of the way in which the grass turns into natural hay by this curing on the stalk.

But scantiness of food, due to overstocking, is the one really great danger to us in the north, who do not have to fear the droughts that occasionally devastate portions of the southern ranges. In a fairly good country, if the feed is plenty, the natural increase of a herd is sure shortly to repair any damage that may be done by an unusually severe winter — unless, indeed, the latter should be one such as occurs but two or three times in a century. When, however, the grass becomes cropped down, then the loss in even an ordinary year is heavy among the weaker animals, and if the winter is at all severe it becomes simply appalling. The snow covers the shorter grass much quicker, and even when there is enough, the cattle, weak and unfit to travel around, have to work hard to get it; their exertions tending to enfeeble them and to render them less able to cope with the exposure and cold. The large patches of brushwood, into which the cattle crowd and which to a small number afford ample shelter and some food, become trodden down and yield neither when the beasts become too plentiful. Again, the grass is, of course, soonest eaten off where there is shelter; and, accordingly, the broken ground to which the animals cling during winter may be grazed bare of vegetation though the open plains, to which only the hardiest will at this season stray, may have plenty; and insufficiency of food, although not such as actually to starve them, weakens them so that they succumb readily to the cold or to one of the numerous accidents to which they are liable — as slipping off an icy butte or getting cast in a frozen washout. The cows in calf are those that suffer most, and so heavy is the loss among these and so light the calf crop that it is yet an open question whether our northern ranges are as a whole fitted for breeding. When the animals get weak they will huddle into some nook or corner and simply stay there till they die. An empty hut, for instance, will often in the spring be found to contain the carcasses of a dozen weak cows or poor steers that have crawled into it for protection from the cold, and once in have never moved out.

Overstocking may cause little or no harm for two or three years, but sooner or later there comes a winter which means ruin to the ranches that have too many cattle on them; and in our country, which is even now getting crowded, it is merely a question of time as to when a winter will come that will understock the ranges by the summary process of killing off about half of all the cattle throughout the North-west.* The herds that have just been put on suffer most in such a case; if they have come on late and are composed of weak animals, very few indeed, perhaps not ten per cent., will survive. The cattle that have been double or single wintered do better; while a range-raised steer is almost as tough as a buffalo.

In our northern country we have "free grass"; that is, the stockmen rarely own more than small portions of the land over which their cattle range, the bulk of it being unsurveyed and still the property of the National Government—for the latter refuses to sell the soil except in small lots, acting on the wise principle of distributing it among as many owners as possible. Here and there some ranchman has acquired title to narrow strips of territory peculiarly valuable as giving water-right; but the amount of land thus occupied is small with us,—although the reverse is the case farther south,—and there is practically no fencing to speak of. As a consequence, the land is one vast pasture, and the man who over-stocks his own range damages his neighbors as much as himself. These huge northern pastures are too dry and the soil too poor to be used for agriculture until the rich, wet lands to the east and west are occupied; and at present we have little to fear from grangers. Of course, in the end much of the ground will be taken up for small farms, but the farmers that so far have come in have absolutely failed to make even a living, except now and then by raising a few vegetables for the use of the stockmen; and we are inclined to welcome the incoming of an occasional settler, if he is a decent man, especially as, by the laws of the Territories in which the great grazing plains lie, he is obliged to fence in his own patch of cleared ground, and we do not have to keep our cattle out of it.

At present we are far more afraid of each other. There are always plenty of men who for the sake of the chance of gain they themselves run are willing to jeopardize the interests of their neighbors by putting on more cattle than the land will support—for the loss, of course, falls as heavily on the man who has put on the right number as on him who has put on too many; and it is against these individuals that we have to guard so far as we are able. To protect ourselves completely is impossi-ble, but the very identity of interest that renders all of us liable to suffer

* Written in the fall of 1886; the ensuing winter exactly fulfilled the prophecy.

BRONCO BUSTERS SADDLING.

for the fault of a few also renders us as a whole able to take some rough measures to guard against the wrong-doing of a portion of our number; for the fact that the cattle wander intermixed over the ranges forces all the ranchmen of a locality to combine if they wish to do their work effectively. Accordingly, the stockmen of a neighborhood, when it holds as many cattle as it safely can, usually unitedly refuse to work with any one who puts in another herd. In the cow country a man is peculiarly dependent upon his neighbors, and a small outfit is wholly unable to work without their assistance when once the cattle have mingled completely with those of other brands. A large outfit is much more master of its destiny, and can do its own work quite by itself; but even such a one can be injured in countless ways if the hostility of the neighboring ranchmen is incurred.

The best days of ranching are over; and though there are many ranchmen who still make money, yet during the past two or three years the majority have certainly lost. This is especially true of the numerous Easterners who went into the business without any experience and trusted themselves entirely to their Western representatives; although, on the other hand, many of those who have made most money at it are Easterners, who, however, have happened to be naturally fitted for the work and who have deliberately settled down to learning the business as they would have learned any other, devoting their whole time and energy to it. Stock-raising, as now carried on, is characteristic of a young and wild land. As the country grows older, it will in some places die out, and in others entirely change its character; the ranches will be broken up, will be gradually modified into stock-farms, or, if on good soil, may even fall under the sway of the husbandman.

In its present form stock-raising on the plains is doomed, and can hardly outlast the century. The great free ranches, with their barbarous, picturesque, and curiously fascinating surroundings, mark a primitive stage of existence as surely as do the great tracts of primeval forests, and like the latter must pass away before the onward march of our people; and we who have felt the charm of the life, and have exulted in its abounding vigor and its bold, restless freedom, will not only regret its passing for our own sakes, but must also feel real sorrow that those who come after us are not to see, as we have seen, what is perhaps the pleasantest, healthiest, and most exciting phase of American existence.

THE HOME RANCH

PONIES PAWING IN THE SNOW.

III

The Home Ranch

Y home ranch lies on both sides of the Little Missouri, the nearest ranchman above me being about twelve, and the nearest below me about ten, miles distant. The general course of the stream here is northerly, but, while flowing through my ranch, it takes a great westerly reach of some three miles, walled in, as always, between chains of steep, high bluffs half a mile or more apart. The stream twists down through the valley in long sweeps, leaving oval wooded bottoms, first on one side and then on the other; and in an open glade among the thick-growing timber stands the long, low house of hewn logs.

Just in front of the ranch veranda is a line of old cottonwoods that shade it during the fierce heats of summer, rendering it always cool and pleasant. But a few feet beyond these trees comes the cut-off bank of the river, through whose broad, sandy bed the shallow stream winds as if lost, except when a freshet fills it from brim to brim with foaming yellow water. The bluffs that wall in the river-valley curve back in semicircles, rising from its alluvial bottom generally as abrupt cliffs, but often as steep, grassy slopes that lead up to great level plateaus; and the line is broken every mile or two by the entrance of a coulee, or dry creek, whose head branches may be twenty miles back. Above us, where the river comes round the bend, the valley is very narrow, and the high buttes bounding it rise, sheer and barren, into scalped hill-peaks and naked knife-blade ridges.

The other buildings stand in the same open glade with the ranch house, the dense growth of cottonwoods and matted, thorny underbrush making a wall all about, through which we have chopped our wagon roads and trodden out our own bridle-paths. The cattle have now trampled down this brush a little, but deer still lie in it, only a couple of hundred yards from the house; and from the door sometimes in the evening one

6

can see them peer out into the open, or make their way down, timidly and cautiously, to drink at the river. The stable, sheds, and other out-buildings, with the hayricks and the pens for such cattle as we bring in during winter, are near the house; the patch of fenced garden land is on the edge of the woods; and near the middle of the glade stands the high, circular horse-corral, with a snubbing-post in the center, and a wing built out from one side of the gate entrance, so that the saddle-band can be driven in without trouble. As it is very hard to work cattle where there is much brush, the larger cow-corral is some four miles off on an open bottom.

A ranchman's life is certainly a very pleasant one, albeit generally varied with plenty of hardship and anxiety. Although occasionally he passes days of severe toil,—for example, if he goes on the round-up he works as hard as any of his men,—yet he no longer has to undergo the monotonous drudgery attendant upon the tasks of the cowboy or of the apprentice in the business. His fare is simple; but, if he chooses, it is good enough. Many ranches are provided with nothing at all but salt pork, canned goods, and bread; indeed, it is a curious fact that in traveling through the cow country it is often impossible to get any milk or butter; but this is only because the owners or managers are too lazy to take enough trouble to insure their own comfort. We ourselves always keep up

ELK HORN RANCH BUILDINGS.

two or three cows, choosing such as are naturally tame, and so we invariably have plenty of milk and, when there is time for churning, a good deal of butter. We also keep hens, which, in spite of the damaging inroads of hawks, bob-cats, and foxes, supply us with eggs, and in time of need, when our rifles have failed to keep us in game, with stewed, roast, or fried chicken also. From our garden we get potatoes, and unless drought, frost, or grasshoppers interfere (which they do about every second year), other vegetables as well. For fresh meat we depend chiefly upon our prowess as hunters.

During much of the time we are away on the different round-ups, that "wheeled house," the great four-horse wagon, being then our home; but when at the ranch our routine of life is always much the same, save during the excessively bitter weather of midwinter, when there is little to do except to hunt, if the days are fine enough. We breakfast early—before dawn when the nights have grown long, and rarely later than sunrise, even in midsummer. Perhaps before this meal, certainly the instant it is over, the man whose duty it is rides off to hunt up and, drive in the saddle-band. Each of us has his own string of horses, eight or ten in number, and the whole band usually split up into two or three companies. In addition to the scattered groups of the saddle-band, our six or eight mares, with their colts, keep by themselves, and are rarely bothered by us, as no cowboy ever rides anything but horses, because mares give great trouble where all the animals have to be herded together. Once every two or three days somebody rides round and finds out where each of these smaller bands is, but the man who goes out in the morning merely gathers one bunch. He drives these into the corral, the other men (who have been lolling idly about the house or stable, fixing their saddles or doing any odd job) coming out with their ropes as soon as they hear the patter of the unshod hoofs and the shouts of the cowboy driver. Going into the corral, and standing near the center, each of us picks out some one of his own string from among the animals that are trotting and running in a compact mass round the circle; and after one or more trials, according to his skill, ropes it and leads it out. When all have caught their horses the rest are again turned loose, together with those that have been kept up overnight. Some horses soon get tame and do not need to be roped; my pet cutting pony, little Muley, and good old Manitou, my companion in so many hunting trips, will neither of them stay with the rest of their fellows that are jamming and jostling each other as they rush round in the dust of the corral, but they very sensibly walk up and stand quietly with the men in the middle, by the snubbing-post. Both are great pets, Manitou in particular; the wise old fellow being very fond of bread and sometimes coming up of his own accord to the ranch house and even putting his head into the door to beg for it.

Once saddled, the men ride off on their different tasks; for almost everything is done in the saddle, except that in winter we cut our fire-wood and quarry our coal,—both on the ranch,—and in summer attend to the garden and put up what wild hay we need.

If any horses have strayed, one or two of the men will be sent off to look for them; for hunting lost horses is one of the commonest and most irksome of our duties. Every outfit always has certain of its horses at large; and if they remain out long enough they become as wild and wary as deer and have to be regularly surrounded and run down. On one occasion, when three of mine had been running loose for a couple of months, we had to follow at full speed for at least fifteen miles before exhausting them enough to enable us to get some control over them and head them towards a corral. Twice I have had horses absent nearly a year before they were recovered. One of them, after being on the ranch nine months, went off one night and traveled about two hundred miles in a straight line back to its old haunts, swimming the Yellowstone on the way. Two others were at one time away nearly eighteen months, during which time we saw them twice, and on one occasion a couple of the men fairly ran their horses down in following them. We began to think they were lost for good, as they were all the time going farther down towards the Sioux country, but we finally recovered them.

If the men do not go horse-hunting they may ride off over the range; for there is generally some work to be done among the cattle, such as driving in and branding calves that have been overlooked by the round-up, or getting some animal out of a bog-hole. During the early spring months, before the round-up begins, the chief work is in hauling out mired cows and steers; and if we did not keep a sharp lookout, the losses at this season would be very serious. As long as everything is frozen solid there is, of course, no danger from miring; but when the thaw comes, along towards the beginning of March, a period of new danger to the cattle sets in. When the ice breaks up, the streams are left with an edging of deep bog, while the quicksand is at its worst. As the frost goes out of the soil, the ground round every little alkali-spring changes into a trembling quagmire, and deep holes of slimy, tenacious mud form in the bottom of all the gullies. The cattle, which have had to live on snow for three or four months, are very eager for water, and are weak and in poor condition. They rush heedlessly into any pool and stand there, drinking gallons of the icy water and sinking steadily into the mud. When they try to get out they are already too deep down, and are too weak to make a prolonged struggle. After one or two fits of desperate floundering, they resign themselves to their fate with dumb apathy and are lost, unless some one of us riding about discovers and hauls them out. They may be thus lost in wonderfully small mud-holes; often they will be found dead in a gulch but two or three feet across, or in the quicksand of a creek so narrow that it could almost be jumped. An alkali-hole, where the water oozes out through the thick clay, is the worst of all, owing to the ropy tenacity with which the horrible substance sticks and clings to any unfortunate beast that gets into it.

In the spring these mud-holes cause very serious losses among the cattle, and are at all times fruitful sources of danger; indeed, during an

ROPING IN A HORSE-CORRAL.

ordinary year more cattle die from getting mired than from any other cause. In addition to this they also often prove very annoying to the rider himself, as getting his steed mired or caught in a quicksand is one of the commonest of the accidents that beset a horseman in the far West. This usually happens in fording a river, if the latter is at all high, or else in crossing one of the numerous creeks; although I once saw a horse and rider suddenly engulfed while leisurely walking over what appeared to be dry land. They had come to an alkali mud-hole, an old buffalo-wallow, which had filled up and was covered with a sun-baked crust, that let them through as if they had stepped on a trap-door. There being several of us along, we got down our ropes and dragged both unfortunates out in short order.

When the river is up it is a very common thing for a horseman to have great difficulty in crossing, for the swift, brown water runs over a bed of deep quicksand that is ever shifting.   An inexperienced horse, or a mule,—for a mule is useless in mud or quicksand,—becomes mad with fright in such a crossing, and, after speedily exhausting its strength in wild struggles, will throw itself on its side and drown unless the rider gets it out.   An old horse used to such work will, on the contrary, take matters quietly and often push along through really dangerous quicksand. Old Manitou never loses his head for an instant; but, now resting a few seconds, now feeling his way cautiously forward, and now making two or three desperate plunges, will go on wherever a horse possibly can.   It is really dangerous crossing some of the creeks, as the bottom may give way where it seems hardest; and if one is alone he may work hours in vain before getting his horse out, even after taking off both saddle and bridle, the only hope being to head it so that every plunge takes it an inch or two in the right direction.

Nor are mud-holes the only danger the horseman has to fear; for in much of the Bad Lands the buttes are so steep and broken that it needs genuine mountaineering skill to get through them, and no horse but a Western one, bred to the business, could accomplish the feat.   In many parts of our country it is impossible for a horseman who does not know the land to cross it, and it is difficult enough even for an experienced hand.   For a stretch of nearly ten miles along the Little Missouri above my range, and where it passes through it, there are but three or four places where it is possible for a horseman to get out to the eastern prairie through the exceedingly broken country lying back from the river.   In places this very rough ground comes down to the water; elsewhere it lies back near the heads of the creeks.   In such very bad ground the whole country seems to be one tangled chaos of canyon-like valleys, winding gullies and washouts with abrupt, unbroken sides, isolated peaks of sandstone, marl, or "gumbo" clay, which rain turns into slippery glue, and hill chains the ridges of which always end in sheer cliffs.   After a man has made his way with infinite toil for half a mile, a point will be reached around which it is an absolute impossibility to go, and the adventurer has nothing to do but painfully retrace his steps and try again in a new direction, as likely as not with the same result.   In such a place the rider dismounts and leads his horse, the latter climbing with cat-like agility up seemingly inaccessible heights, scrambling across the steep, sloping shoulders of the bluffs, sliding down the faces of the clay cliffs with all four legs rigid, or dropping from ledge to ledge like a goat, and accepting with unruffled composure an occasional roll from top to bottom. But, in spite of the climbing abilities of the ponies, it is difficult, and at times—for our steeds, at any rate—dangerous work to go through such places, and we only do it when it cannot be avoided. Once I was over-taken by darkness while trying to get through a great tract of very rough land, and, after once or twice nearly breaking my neck, in despair had to give up all attempts to get out, and until daybreak simply staid where I was, in a kind of ledge or pocket on the side of the cliff, luckily sheltered from the wind. It was midsummer and the nights were short, but this particular one seemed quite long enough; and though I was on the move by dawn, it was three hours later before I led the horse, as hungry, numb, and stiff as myself, out on the prairie again.

Occasionally it is imperatively necessary to cross some of the worst parts of the Bad Lands with a wagon, and such a trip is exhausting and laborious beyond belief. Often the wagon will have to be taken to pieces every few hundred yards in order to get it over a ravine, lower it into a valley, or drag it up a cliff. One outfit, that a year ago tried to take a short cut through some of the Bad Lands of the Powder River, made just four miles in three days, and then had to come back to their starting-point after all. But with only saddle-horses we feel that it must be a very extraordinary country indeed if, in case of necessity, we cannot go through it.

The long forenoon's work, with its attendant mishaps to man and beast, being over, the men who have been out among the horses and cattle come riding in, to be joined by their fellows—if any there be—who have been hunting, or haying, or chopping wood. The midday dinner is variable as to time, for it comes when the men have returned from their work; but, whatever be the hour, it is the most substantial meal of the day, and we feel that we have little fault to find with a table on the clean cloth of which are spread platters of smoked elk meat, loaves of good bread, jugs and bowls of milk, saddles of venison or broiled antelope steaks, perhaps roast and fried prairie chickens, with eggs, butter, wild plums, and tea or coffee.

The afternoon's tasks are usually much the same as the morning's, but this time is often spent in doing the odds and ends; as, for instance, it may be devoted to breaking-in a new horse. Large outfits gener-ally hire a bronco-buster to do this; but we ourselves almost always break our own horses, two or three of my men being pretty good riders, although none of them can claim to be anything out of the common. A first-class flash rider or bronco-buster receives high wages, and deserves them, for he follows a most dangerous trade, at which no man can hope to grow old ; his work being infinitely harder than that of an Eastern horse-breaker or rough-rider, because he has to do it in such a limited time.   A good rider is a good rider all the world over ; but an Eastern or English horse-breaker and Western bronco-buster have so little in common with each other as regards style or surroundings, and are so totally out of place in doing each other's work, that it is almost impossible to get either to admit that the other has any merits at all as a horseman, for neither could sit in the saddle of the other or could without great difficulty per-form his task.   The ordinary Eastern seat, which approaches more or less

A DEEP FORD.

the seat of a cross-country rider or fox-hunter, is nearly as different from the cowboy's seat as from that of a man who rides bareback.   The stir-rups on a stock saddle are much farther back than they are on an ordinary English one (a difference far more important than the high horn and cantle of the former), and the man stands nearly erect in them, instead of having his legs bent ; and he grips with the thighs and not with the knees, throwing his feet well out.   Some of the things he teaches his horse would be wholly useless to an Eastern equestrian : for example, one of the first lessons the newly-caught animal has to learn is not to "run on a rope"; and he is taught this by being violently snubbed up, probably turning a somersault, the first two or three times that he feels the noose settle round his neck, and makes a mad rush for liberty. The snubbing-post is the usual adjunct in teaching such a lesson; but a skillful man can do without any help and throw a horse clean over by holding the rope tight against the left haunch, at the same time leaning so far back, with the legs straight in front, that the heels dig deep into the ground when the strain comes, and the horse, running out with the slack of the rope, is brought up standing, or even turned head over heels by the shock. Cowboys are probably the only working-men in the world who invariably wear gloves, buckskin gauntlets being preferred, as otherwise the ropes would soon take every particle of skin off their hands.

A bronco-buster has to work by such violent methods in consequence of the short amount of time at his command. Horses are cheap, each outfit has a great many, and the wages for breaking an animal are but five or ten dollars. Three rides, of an hour or two each, on as many consecutive days, are the outside number a bronco-buster deems necessary before turning an animal over as "broken." The average bronco-buster, however, handles horses so very rudely that we prefer, aside from motives of economy, to break our own; and this is always possible, if we take enough time. The best and quietest horses on the ranch are far from being those broken by the best riders; on the contrary, they are those that have been handled most gently, although firmly, and that have had the greatest number of days devoted to their education.

Some horses, of course, are almost incurably vicious, and must be conquered by main force. One pleasing brute on my ranch will at times rush at a man open-mouthed like a wolf, and this is a regular trick of the range-stallions. In a great many—indeed, in most—localities there are wild horses to be found, which, although invariably of domestic descent, being either themselves runaways from some ranch or Indian outfit, or else claiming such for their sires and dams, yet are quite as wild as the antelope on whose domain they have intruded. Ranchmen run in these wild horses whenever possible, and they are but little more difficult to break than the so-called "tame" animals. But the wild stallions are, whenever possible, shot; both because of their propensity for driving off the ranch mares, and because their incurable viciousness makes them always unsafe companions for other horses still more than for men. A wild stallion fears no beast except the grizzly, and will not always flinch from an encounter with it; yet it is a curious fact that a jack will almost always kill one in a fair fight. The particulars of a fight of this sort were related to me by a cattle man who was engaged in bringing out blooded stock from the East. Among the animals under his charge were two great stallions, one gray and one black, and a fine jackass, not much over half the size of either of the former. The animals were kept in separate pens, but one day both horses got into the same inclosure, next to the jack-pen, and began to fight as only enraged stallions can, striking like boxers

with their fore feet, and biting with their teeth. The gray was getting the best of it; but while clinched with his antagonist in one tussle they rolled against the jack-pen, breaking it in. No sooner was the jack at liberty than, with ears laid back and mouth wide open, he made straight for the two horses, who had for the moment separated.

A HARD TRAIL.

The gray turned to meet him, rearing on his hind legs and striking at him with his fore feet; but the jack slipped in, and in a minute grasped his antagonist by the throat with his wide-open jaws, and then held on like a bull-dog, all four feet planted stiffly in the soil.   The stallion made tremendous efforts to shake him off: he would try to whirl round and kick him, but for that the jack was too short; then he would rise up, lifting the jack off the ground, and strike at him with his fore feet; but all that he gained by this was to skin his foe's front legs without making him loose his hold.   Twice they fell, and twice the stallion rose, by main strength dragging the jack with him; but all in vain.   Meanwhile the black horse attacked both the combatants, with perfect impartiality, striking and kicking them with his hoofs, while his teeth, as they slipped off the tough hides, met with a snap like that of a bear-trap.   Undoubtedly the jack would have killed at least one of the horses had not the men come up, and with no small difficulty separated the maddened brutes.

If not breaking horses, mending saddles, or doing something else of the sort, the cowboys will often while away their leisure moments by practicing with the rope.   A man cannot practice too much with this if he wishes to attain even moderate proficiency; and as a matter of fact he soon gets to wish to practice the whole time.   A cowboy is always roping something, and it especially delights him to try his skill at game. A friend of mine, a young ranchman in the Judith basin, about four years ago roped a buffalo, and by the exercise of the greatest skill, both on his own part and on his steed's, actually succeeded, by alternate bullying and coaxing, in getting the huge brute almost into camp.   I have occasionally known men on fast horses to rope deer, and even antelope, when circumstances all joined to favor them; and last summer one of the cowboys on a ranch about thirty miles off ran into and roped a wounded elk.   A forty-foot lariat is the one commonly used, for the ordinary range at which a man can throw it is only about twenty-five feet.   Few men can throw forty feet; and to do this, taking into account the coil, needs a sixty-foot rope.

When the day's work is over we take supper, and bed-time comes soon afterward, for the men who live on ranches sleep well and soundly.   As a rule, the nights are cool and bracing, even in midsummer; except when we occasionally have a spell of burning weather, with a steady, hot wind that blows in our faces like a furnace blast, sending the thermometer far up above a hundred and making us gasp for breath, even at night, in the dry-baked heat of the air.   But it is only rarely that we get a few days of this sort; generally, no matter how unbearable the heat of the day has been, we can at least sleep pleasantly at night.

A ranchman's work is, of course, free from much of the sameness attendant upon that of a mere cowboy. One day he will ride out with his men among the cattle, or after strayed horses; the next he may hunt, so as to keep the ranch in meat; then he can make the tour of his out-lying camps; or, again, may join one of the round-ups for a week or two, perhaps keeping with it the entire time it is working. On occasions he will have a good deal of spare time on his hands, which, if he chooses, he can spend in reading or writing. If he cares for books, there will be many a worn volume in the primitive little sitting-room, with its log walls and huge fire-place; but after a hard day's work a man will not read much, but will rock to and fro in the flickering firelight, talking sleepily over his success in the day's chase and the difficulty he has had with the cattle; or else may simply lie stretched at full length on the elk-hides and wolf-skins in front of the hearthstone, listening in drowsy silence to the roar and crackle of the blazing logs and to the moaning of the wind outside.

In the sharp fall weather the riding is delicious all day long; but even in the late spring, and all through the summer, we try, if we can, to do our work before the heat of the day, and if going on a long ride, whether to hunt or for other purposes, leave the ranch house by dawn.

The early rides in the spring mornings have a charm all their own, for they are taken when, for the one and only time during the year, the same brown landscape of these high plains turns to a vivid green, as the new grass sprouts and the trees and bushes thrust forth the young leaves; and at dawn, with the dew glittering everywhere, all things show at their best and freshest. The flowers are out and a man may gallop for miles at a stretch with his horse's hoofs sinking at every stride into the carpet of prairie roses, whose short stalks lift the beautiful blossoms but a few inches from the ground. Even in the waste places the cactuses are blooming; and one kind in particular, a dwarfish, globular plant, with its mass of splendid crimson flowers glows against the sides of the gray buttes like a splash of flame.

The ravines, winding about and splitting into a labyrinth of coulees, with chains of rounded hills to separate them, have groves of trees in their bottoms, along the sides of the water courses. In these are found the blacktail deer, and his cousin, the whitetail, too, with his flaunting flag; but in the spring-time, when we are after antelope only, we must go out farther to the flat prairie land on the divide. Here, in places, the level, grassy plains are strewn with mounds and hillocks of red or gray scoria, that stand singly or clustered into little groups, their tops crested, or their sides covered, by queer detached masses of volcanic rock, wrought into strange shapes by the dead forces whose blind, hidden strength long ago called them into being. The road our wagons take, when the water is too high for us to come down the river bottom, stretches far ahead—two dark,

IN WITH THE HORSE HERD.

straight, parallel furrows which merge into one in the distance. Quaint little horned frogs crawl sluggishly along in the wheel tracks, and the sickle-billed curlews run over the ground or soar above and around the horsemen, uttering their mournful, never-ceasing clamor. The grass-land stretches out in the sunlight like a sea, every wind bending the blades into a ripple, and flecking the prairie with shifting patches of a different green from that around, exactly as the touch of a light squall or wind-gust will fleck the smooth surface of the ocean. Our Western plains differ widely in detail from those of Asia; yet they always call to mind

> .   .   .   .   The Scythian
> On the wide steppe, unharnessing
> His wheel'd house at noon.
> He tethers his beast down, and makes his meal —
> Mares' milk, and bread
> Baked on the embers; — all around
> The boundless, waving grass-plains stretch   .   .   .
> .   .   .; before him, for long miles,
> Alive with bright green lizards
> And the springing bustard fowl,
> The track, a straight black line,
> Furrows the rich soil; here and there
> Clusters of lonely mounds
> Topp'd with rough hewn,
> Gray, rain-blear'd statues, overpeer
> The sunny waste.

In the spring mornings the rider on the plains will hear bird songs unknown in the East. The Missouri skylark sings while soaring above the great plateaus so high in the air that it is impossible to see the bird; and this habit of singing while soaring it shares with some sparrow-like birds that are often found in company with it. The white-shouldered lark-bunting, in its livery of black, has rich, full notes, and as it sings on the wing it reminds one of the bobolink; and the sweet-voiced lark-finch also utters its song in the air. These birds, and most of the sparrows of the plains, are characteristic of this region.

But many of our birds, especially those found in the wooded river bottoms, answer to those of the East; only almost each one has some marked point of difference from its Eastern representative. The bluebird out West is very much of a blue bird indeed, for it has no "earth tinge" on its breast at all; while the indigo-bird, on the contrary, has gained the ruddy markings that the other has lost. The flicker has the shafts of its wing and tail quills colored orange instead of yellow. The towhee has lost all title to its name, for its only cry is a mew like that of a cat-bird; while, most wonderful of all, the meadow-lark has found a rich, strong voice, and is one of the sweetest and most incessant singers we have.

Throughout June the thickets and groves about the ranch house are loud with bird music from before dawn till long after sunrise. The thrashers have sung all the night through from among the thorn-bushes if there has been a moon, or even if there has been bright starlight; and before the first glimmer of gray the bell-like, silvery songs of the shy woodland thrushes chime in; while meadow-lark, robin, bluebird, and song sparrow, together with many rarer singers, like the grosbeak, join in swelling the chorus. There are some would-be singers whose intention is better than their execution. Blackbirds of several kinds are plenty round the house and stables, walking about with a knowing air, like so many dwarf crows; and now and then a flock of yellow-heads will mix for a few days with their purple or rusty-colored brethren. The males of these yellow-headed grakles are really handsome, their orange and yellow heads contrasting finely with the black of the rest of their plumage; but their voices are discordant to a degree. When a flock has done feeding it will often light in straggling order among the trees in front of the veranda, and then the males will begin to sing, or rather to utter the most extraordinary collection of broken sounds—creakings, gurglings, hisses, twitters, and every now and then a liquid note or two. It is like an accentuated representation of the noise made by a flock of common black-birds. At nightfall the poor-wills begin to utter their boding call from the wooded ravines back in the hills; not "whip-poor-will," as in the East, but with two syllables only. They often come round the ranch house. Late one evening I had been sitting motionless on the veranda, looking out across the water and watching the green and brown of the hill-tops change to purple and umber and then fade off into shadowy gray as the somber darkness deepened. Suddenly a poor-will lit on the floor beside me and stayed some little time; now and then uttering its mournful cries, then ceasing for a few moments as it flitted round after insects, and again returning to the same place to begin anew. The little owls, too, call to each other with tremulous, quavering voices throughout the livelong night, as they sit in the creaking trees that overhang the roof. Now and then we hear the wilder voices of the wilderness, from animals that in the hours of darkness do not fear the neighborhood of man: the coyotes wail like dismal ventriloquists, or the silence may be broken by the strident challenge of a lynx, or by the snorting and stamping of a deer that has come to the edge of the open.

In the hot noontide hours of midsummer the broad ranch veranda, always in the shade, is almost the only spot where a man can be comfortable; but here he can sit for hours at a time, leaning back in his rocking-chair, as he reads or smokes, or with half-closed, dreamy eyes gazes across the shallow, nearly dry river-bed to the wooded bottoms opposite, and to the plateaus lying back of them. Against the sheer white faces of the cliffs, that come down without a break, the dark green tree-tops stand out in bold relief. In the hot, lifeless air all objects that are not near by seem to sway and waver. There are few sounds to break the stillness. From the upper branches of the cottonwood trees overhead, whose shimmering, tremulous leaves are hardly ever quiet, but if the wind stirs at all, rustle and quiver and sigh all day long, comes every now and then the soft, melancholy cooing of the mourning dove, whose voice always seems

A BUCKING BRONCO.

far away and expresses more than any other sound in nature the sadness of gentle, hopeless, never-ending grief. The other birds are still; and very few animals move about. Now and then the black shadow of a wheeling vulture falls on the sun-scorched ground. The cattle, that have strung down in long files from the hills, lie quietly on the sand-bars, except that some of the bulls keep traveling up and down, bellowing and routing or giving vent to long, surly grumblings as they paw the sand and toss it up with their horns. At times the horses, too, will come down to drink, and to splash and roll in the water.

The prairie-dogs alone are not daunted by the heat, but sit at the mouths of their burrows with their usual pert curiosity. They are bothersome little fellows, and most prolific, increasing in spite of the perpetual war made on them by every carnivorous bird and beast. One of their worst foes is the black-footed ferret, a handsome, rather rare animal, somewhat like a mink, with a yellow-brown body and dark feet and mask. It is a most bloodthirsty little brute, feeding on all small animals and ground birds. It will readily master a jack-rabbit, will kill very young fawns if it finds them in the mother's absence, and works extraordinary havoc in a dog town, as it can follow the wretched little beasts down into the burrows. In one instance, I knew of a black-footed ferret making a succession of inroads on a ranchman's poultry, killing and carrying off most of them before it was trapped. Coyotes, foxes, swifts, badgers, and skunks also like to lurk about the dog towns. Of the skunks, by the way, we had last year altogether too much; there was a perfect plague of them all along the river, and they took to trying to get into the huts, with the stupid pertinacity of the species. At every ranch house dozens were killed, we ourselves bagging thirty-three, all slain near the house, and one, to our unspeakable sorrow, in it.

In making a journey over ground we know, during the hot weather we often prefer to ride by moonlight. The moon shines very brightly through the dry, clear night air, turning the gray buttes into glimmering silver; and the horses travel far more readily and easily than under the glaring noonday sun. The road between my upper and lower ranch houses is about forty miles long, sometimes following the river-bed, and then again branching off inland, crossing the great plateaus and winding through the ravines of the broken country. It is a five-hours' fair ride; and so, in a hot spell, we like to take it during the cool of the night, starting at sunset. After nightfall the face of the country seems to alter marvelously, and the clear moonlight only intensifies the change. The river gleams like running quicksilver, and the moonbeams play over the grassy stretches of the plateaus and glance off the wind-rippled blades as they would from water. The Bad Lands seem to be stranger and wilder than ever, the silvery rays turning the country into a kind of grim fairy-

8

land. The grotesque, fantastic outlines of the higher cliffs stand out with startling clearness, while the lower buttes have become formless, misshapen masses, and the deep gorges are in black shadow; in the darkness there will be no sound but the rhythmic echo of the hoof-beats of the horses, and the steady, metallic clank of the steel bridle-chains.

But the fall is the time for riding; for in the keen, frosty air neither man nor beast will tire, though out from the dawn until the shadows have again waxed long and the daylight has begun to wane, warning all to push straight for home without drawing rein. Then deer-saddles and elk-haunches hang from the trees near the house; and one can have good sport right on the sand of the river-bed, for we always keep shot-gun or rifle at hand, to be ready for any prairie chickens, or for such of the passing water-fowl as light in the river near us. Occasionally we take a shot at a flock of waders, among which the pretty avocets are the most striking in looks and manners. Prairie fowl are quite plenty all round us, and occasionally small flocks come fairly down into the yard, or perch among the trees near by. At evening they fly down to the river to drink, and as they sit on the sand-bars offer fine marks for the rifles. So do the geese and ducks when they occasionally light on the same places or paddle leisurely down stream in the middle of the river; but to make much of a bag of these we have to use the heavy No. 10, choke-bore shot-gun, while the little 16-bore fowling-piece is much the handiest for prairie fowl. A good many different kinds of water-fowl pass, ranging in size from a teal duck to a Canada goose, and all of them at times help to eke out our bill of fare. Last fall a white-fronted goose lighted on the river in front of the ranch house, and three of us, armed with miscellaneous weapons, went out after him; we disabled him, and then after much bad shooting, and more violent running through thick sand and thick underbrush, finally overtook and most foully butchered him. The snow geese and common wild geese are what we usually kill, however.

Sometimes strings of sandbill cranes fly along the river, their guttural clangor being heard very far off. They usually light on a plateau, where sometimes they form rings and go through a series of queer antics, dancing and posturing to each other. They are exceedingly wide-awake birds, and more shy and wary than antelope, so that they are rarely shot; yet once I succeeded in stalking up to a group in the early morning, and firing into them rather at random, my bullet killed a full-grown female. Its breast, when roasted, proved to be very good eating.

Sometimes we vary our diet with fish—wall-eyed pike, ugly, slimy catfish, and other uncouth finny things, looking very fit denizens of the mud-choked water; but they are good eating withal, in spite of their uncanny appearance. We usually catch them with set lines, left out over-night in the deeper pools.

CRUISING FOR STOCK.

The cattle are fattest and in best condition during the fall, and it is then that the bulk of the beef steers are gathered and shipped—four-year-olds as a rule, though some threes and fives go along with them. Cattle are a nuisance while hunting on foot, as they either take fright and run off when they see the hunter, scaring all game within sight, or else, what is worse, follow him, blustering and bullying and pretending that they are on the point of charging, but rarely actually doing so. Still, they are occasionally really dangerous, and it is never entirely safe for a man to be on foot when there is a chance of meeting the droves of long-horned steers. But they will always bluster rather than fight, whether with men or beasts, or with one another. The bulls and some of the steers are for-ever traveling and challenging each other, never ceasing their hoarse rumbling and moaning and their long-drawn, savage bellowing, tearing up the banks with their horns and sending little spurts of dust above their shoulders with their fore hoofs; yet they do not seem especially fond of real fighting, although, of course, they do occasionally have most desperate and obstinate set-tos with one another. A large bear will make short work of a bull: a few months ago one of the former killed a very big bull near a ranch house a score of miles or so distant, and during one night tore up and devoured a large part of his victim. The ranchman poisoned the carcass and killed the bear.

OLD-STYLE TEXAN COWMAN.

THE ROUND-UP

BRONCOS AND TIMBER WOLVES.

IV

The Round-Up

DURING the winter-time there is ordinarily but little work done among the cattle. There is some line riding, and a continual lookout is kept for the very weak animals,— usually cows and calves, who have to be driven in, fed, and housed; but most of the stock are left to shift for themselves, undisturbed. Almost every stock-growers' association forbids branding any calves before the spring round-up. If great bands of cattle wander off the range, parties may be fitted out to go after them and bring them back; but this is only done when absolutely necessary, as when the drift of the cattle has been towards an Indian reservation or a settled granger country, for the weather is very severe, and the horses are so poor that their food must be carried along.

The bulk of the work is done during the summer, including the late spring and early fall, and consists mainly in a succession of round-ups, beginning, with us, in May and ending towards the last of October.

But a good deal may be done in the intervals by riding over one's range. Frequently, too, herding will be practiced on a large scale.

Still more important is the "trail" work; cattle, while driven from one range to another, or to a shipping point for beef, being said to be "on the trail." For years, the over-supply from the vast breeding ranches to the south, especially in Texas, has been driven northward in large herds, either to the shipping towns along the great railroads, or else to the fattening ranges of the North-west; it having been found, so far, that while the calf crop is larger in the South, beeves become much heavier in the North. Such cattle, for the most part, went along tolerably well-marked routes or trails, which became for the time being of great importance, flourishing—and extremely lawless—towns growing up along them; but with the growth of the railroad system, and above all with the filling-up of the northern ranges, these trails have steadily become of less and less consequence, though many herds still travel them on their way to the already crowded ranges of western Dakota and Montana, or to the Canadian regions beyond. The trail work is something by itself. The herds may be on the trail several months, averaging fifteen miles or less a day. The cowboys accompanying each have to undergo much hard toil, of a peculiarly same and wearisome kind, on account of the extreme slowness with which everything must be done, as trail cattle should never be hurried. The foreman of a trail outfit must be not only a veteran cowhand, but also a miracle of patience and resolution.

Round-up work is far less irksome, there being an immense amount of dash and excitement connected with it; and when once the cattle are on the range, the important work is done during the round-up. On cow ranches, or wherever there is breeding stock, the spring round-up is the great event of the season, as it is then that the bulk of the calves are branded. It usually lasts six weeks, or thereabouts; but its end by no means implies rest for the stockman. On the contrary, as soon as it is over, wagons are sent to work out-of-the-way parts of the country that have been passed over, but where cattle are supposed to have drifted; and by the time these have come back the first beef round-up has begun, and thereafter beeves are steadily gathered and shipped, at least from among the larger herds, until cold weather sets in; and in the fall there is another round-up, to brand the late calves and see that the stock is got back on the range. As all of these round-ups are of one character, a description of the most important, taking place in the spring, will be enough.

In April we begin to get up the horses. Throughout the winter very few have been kept for use, as they are then poor and weak, and must be given grain and hay if they are to be worked. The men in the line camps need two or three apiece, and each man at the home ranch has a couple more; but the rest are left out to shift for themselves, which the tough, hardy little fellows are well able to do. Ponies can pick up a living where cattle die; though the scanty feed, which they may have to uncover by pawing off the snow, and the bitter weather often make them look very gaunt by spring-time. But the first warm rains bring up the green grass, and then all the live-stock gain flesh with wonderful rapidity. When the spring round-up begins the horses should be as fat and sleek as possible. After running all winter free, even the most sober pony is apt to betray an inclination to buck; and, if possible, we like to ride every animal once or twice before we begin to do real work with him. Animals that have escaped for any length of time are almost as bad to handle as if they had never been broken. One of the two horses mentioned in a former chapter as having been gone eighteen months has, since his return, been suggestively dubbed "Dynamite Jimmy," on account of the incessant and eruptive energy with which he bucks. Many of our horses, by the way, are thus named from some feat or peculiarity. Wire Fence, when being broken, ran into one of the abominations after which he is now called; Hackamore once got away and remained out for three weeks with a hackamore, or breaking-halter, on him; Macaulay contracted the habit of regularly getting rid of the huge Scotchman to whom he was intrusted; Bulberry Johnny spent the hour or two after he was first mounted in a large patch of thorny bulberry bushes, his distracted rider unable to get him to do anything but move round sidewise in a circle; Fall Back would never get to the front; Water Skip always jumps mud-puddles; and there are a dozen others with names as purely descriptive.

The stock-growers of Montana, of the western part of Dakota, and even of portions of extreme northern Wyoming,—that is, of all the grazing lands lying in the basin of the Upper Missouri,—have united, and formed themselves into the great Montana Stock-growers' Association. Among the countless benefits they have derived from this course, not the least has been the way in which the various round-ups work in with and supplement one another. At the spring meeting of the association, the entire territory mentioned above, including perhaps a hundred thousand square miles, is mapped out into round-up districts, which generally are changed but slightly from year to year, and the times and places for the round-ups to begin refixed so that those of adjacent districts may be run with a view to the best interests of all. Thus the stockmen along the Yellowstone have one round-up; we along the Little Missouri have another; and the country lying between, through which the Big Beaver flows, is almost equally important to both. Accordingly, one spring, the Little Missouri round-up, beginning May 25, and working down-stream, was timed so as to reach the mouth of the Big Beaver about June 1, the Yellowstone round-up beginning at that date and place. Both then worked up the Beaver together to its head, when the Yellowstone men turned to the west and we bent back to our own river; thus the bulk of the strayed cattle of each were brought back to their respective ranges. Our own round-up district covers the Big and Little Beaver creeks, which rise near each other, but empty into the Little Missouri nearly a hundred and fifty miles apart, and so much of the latter river as lies between their mouths.

The captain or foreman of the round-up, upon whom very much of its efficiency and success depends, is chosen beforehand. He is, of course,

9

an expert cowman, thoroughly acquainted with the country; and he must also be able to command and to keep control of the wild rough-riders he has under him—a feat needing both tact and firmness.

At the appointed day all meet at the place from which the round-up is to start. Each ranch, of course, has most work to be done in its own round-up district, but it is also necessary to have representatives in all those surrounding it. A large outfit may employ a dozen cowboys, or over, in the home district, and yet have nearly as many more representing its interest in the various ones adjoining. Smaller outfits generally club together to run a wagon and send outside representatives, or else go along with their stronger neighbors, they paying part of the expenses. A large outfit, with a herd of twenty thousand cattle or more, can, if necessary, run a round-up entirely by itself, and is able to act independently of outside help; it is therefore at a great advantage compared with those that can take no step effectively without their neighbors' consent and assistance.

If the starting-point is some distance off, it may be necessary to leave home three or four days in advance. Before this we have got everything in readiness; have overhauled the wagons, shod any horse whose forefeet are tender,—as a rule, all our ponies go barefooted,—and left things in order at the ranch. Our outfit may be taken as a sample of every one else's. We have a stout four-horse wagon to carry the bedding and the food; in its rear a mess-chest is rigged to hold the knives, forks, cans, etc. All our four team-horses are strong, willing animals, though of no great size, being originally just "broncos," or unbroken native horses, like the others. The teamster is also cook: a man who is a really first-rate hand at both driving and cooking—and our present teamster is both—can always command his price. Besides our own men, some cowboys from neighboring ranches and two or three representatives from other round-up districts are always along, and we generally have at least a dozen "riders," as they are termed,—that is, cowboys, or "cow-punchers," who do the actual cattle-work,—with the wagon. Each of these has a string of eight or ten ponies; and to take charge of the saddle-band, thus consisting of a hundred odd head, there are two herders, always known as "horse-wranglers"—one for the day and one for the night. Occasionally there will be two wagons, one to carry the bedding and one the food, known, respectively, as the bed and the mess wagon; but this is not usual.

While traveling to the meeting-point the pace is always slow, as it is an object to bring the horses on the ground as fresh as possible. Accordingly we keep at a walk almost all day, and the riders, having nothing else to do, assist the wranglers in driving the saddle-band, three or four going in front, and others on the side, so that the horses shall keep on a walk. There is always some trouble with the animals at the starting out, as they are very fresh and are restive under the saddle. The herd is

DRIVING TO THE ROUND-UP.

likely to stampede, and any beast that is frisky or vicious is sure to show its worst side. To do really effective cow-work a pony should be well broken; but many even of the old ones have vicious traits, and almost every man will have in his string one or two young horses, or broncos, hardly broken at all. Thanks to the rough methods of breaking in vogue on the plains many even of the so-called broken animals retain always certain bad habits, the most common being that of bucking. Of the sixty odd horses on my ranch all but half a dozen were broken by ourselves; and though my men are all good riders, yet a good rider is not necessarily a good horse-breaker, and indeed it was an absolute impossibility properly to break so many animals in the short time at our command—for we had to use them almost immediately after they were bought. In consequence, very many of my horses have to this day traits not likely to set a timid or a clumsy rider at his ease. One or two run away and cannot be held by even the strongest bit; others can hardly be bridled or saddled until they have been thrown; two or three have a tendency to fall over backward; and half of them buck more or less, some so hard that only an expert can sit them; several I never ride myself, save from dire necessity.

In riding these wild, vicious horses, and in careering over such very bad ground, especially at night, accidents are always occurring. A man who is merely an ordinary rider is certain to have a pretty hard time. On my first round-up I had a string of nine horses, four of them broncos, only broken to the extent of having each been saddled once or twice. One of them it was an impossibility to bridle or to saddle single-handed; it was very difficult to get on or off him, and he was exceedingly nervous if a man moved his hands or feet; but he had no bad tricks. The second soon became perfectly quiet. The third turned out to be one of the worst buckers on the ranch: once, when he bucked me off, I managed to fall on a stone and broke a rib. The fourth had a still worse habit, for he would balk and then throw himself over backward: once, when I was not quick enough, he caught me and broke something in the point of my shoulder, so that it was some weeks before I could raise the arm freely. My hurts were far from serious, and did not interfere with my riding and working as usual through the round-up; but I was heartily glad when it ended, and ever since have religiously done my best to get none but gentle horses in my own string. However, every one gets falls from or with his horse now and then in the cow country; and even my men, good riders though they are, are sometimes injured. One of them once broke his ankle; another a rib; another was on one occasion stunned, remaining unconscious for some hours; and yet another had certain of his horses buck under him so hard and long as finally to hurt his lungs and make him cough blood. Fatal accidents occur annually in almost every district, especially if there is much work to be done among stampeded cattle at night; but on my own ranch none of my men have ever been seriously hurt, though on one occasion a cowboy from another ranch, who was with my wagon, was killed, his horse falling and pitching him heavily on his head.

For bedding, each man has two or three pairs of blankets, and a tarpaulin or small wagon-sheet. Usually, two or three sleep together. Even in June the nights are generally cool and pleasant, and it is chilly

in the early mornings; although this is not always so, and when the
weather stays hot and mosquitoes are plenty, the hours of darkness, even
in midsummer, seem painfully long.   In the Bad Lands proper we are
not often bothered very seriously by these winged pests; but in the low
bottoms of the Big Missouri, and beside many of the reedy ponds and
great sloughs out on the prairie, they are a perfect scourge.   During the
very hot nights, when they are especially active, the bed-clothes make
a man feel absolutely smothered, and yet his only chance for sleep is
to wrap himself tightly up, head and all; and even then some of the
pests will usually force their way in.   At sunset I have seen the mosquitoes rise up from the land like a dense cloud, to make the hot, stifling
night one long torture; the horses would neither lie down nor graze,
traveling restlessly to and fro till daybreak, their bodies streaked and
bloody, and the insects settling on them so as to make them all one color,
a uniform gray; while the men, after a few hours' tossing about in the
vain attempt to sleep, rose, built a little fire of damp sage brush, and thus
endured the misery as best they could until it was light enough to work.

But if the weather is fine, a man will never sleep better nor more
pleasantly than in the open air after a hard day's work on the round-up;
nor will an ordinary shower or gust of wind disturb him in the least, for
he simply draws the tarpaulin over his head and goes on sleeping.   But
now and then we have a wind-storm that might better be called a whirl-
wind and has to be met very differently; and two or three days or nights
of rain insure the wetting of the blankets, and therefore shivering discomfort on the part of the would-be sleeper.   For two or three hours all
goes well; and it is rather soothing to listen to the steady patter of the
great raindrops on the canvas.   But then it will be found that a corner has
been left open through which the water can get in, or else the tarpaulin
will begin to leak somewhere; or perhaps the water will have collected
in a hollow underneath and have begun to soak through.   Soon a little
stream trickles in, and every effort to remedy matters merely results in a
change for the worse.   To move out of the way insures getting wet in a
fresh spot; and the best course is to lie still and accept the evils that
have come with what fortitude one can.   Even thus, the first night a man
can sleep pretty well; but if the rain continues, the second night, when
the blankets are already damp, and when the water comes through more
easily, is apt to be most unpleasant.

Of course, a man can take little spare clothing on a round-up; at the
very outside two or three clean handkerchiefs, a pair of socks, a change
of underclothes, and the most primitive kind of washing-apparatus, all

wrapped up in a stout jacket which is to be worn when night-herding. The inevitable "slicker," or oil-skin coat, which gives complete protection from the wet, is always carried behind the saddle.

SADDLING FRESH HORSES.

At the meeting-place there is usually a delay of a day or two to let every one come in; and the plain on which the encampment is made becomes a scene of great bustle and turmoil. The heavy four-horse wagons jolt in from different quarters, the horse-wranglers rushing madly to and fro in the endeavor to keep the different saddle-bands from mingling, while the "riders," or cowboys, with each wagon jog along in a body. The representatives from outside districts ride in singly or by twos and threes, every man driving before him his own horses, one of them loaded with his bedding. Each wagon wheels out of the way into some camping-place not too near the others, the bedding is tossed out on the ground, and then every one is left to do what he wishes, while the different wagon bosses, or foremen, seek out the captain of the round-up to learn what his plans are.

There is a good deal of rough but effective discipline and method in the way in which a round-up is carried on. The captain of the whole has as lieutenants the various wagon foremen, and in making demands for men to do some special service he will usually merely designate some foreman to take charge of the work and let him parcel it out among his men to suit himself. The captain of the round-up or the foreman of a wagon may himself be a ranchman; if such is not the case, and the ranchman nevertheless comes along, he works and fares precisely as do the other cowboys.

While the head men are gathered in a little knot, planning out the work, the others are dispersed over the plain in every direction, racing, breaking rough horses, or simply larking with one another. If a man has an especially bad horse, he usually takes such an opportunity, when he has plenty of time, to ride him; and while saddling he is surrounded by a crowd of most unsympathetic associates who greet with uproarious mirth any misadventure. A man on a bucking horse is always considered fair game, every squeal and jump of the bronco being hailed with cheers of delighted irony for the rider and shouts to "stay with him." The antics of a vicious bronco show infinite variety of detail, but are all modeled on one general plan. When the rope settles round his neck the fight begins, and it is only after much plunging and snorting that a twist is taken over his nose, or else a hackamore—a species of severe halter, usually made of plaited hair—slipped on his head. While being bridled he strikes viciously with his fore feet, and perhaps has to be blindfolded or thrown down; and to get the saddle on him is quite as difficult. When saddled, he may get rid of his exuberant spirits by bucking under the saddle, or may reserve all his energies for the rider. In the last case, the man keeping tight hold with his left hand of the cheek-strap, so as to prevent the horse from getting his head down until he is fairly seated, swings himself quickly into the saddle. Up rises the bronco's back into an arch; his head, the ears laid straight back, goes down between his forefeet, and, squealing savagely, he makes a succession of rapid, stiff-legged, jarring bounds. Sometimes he is a "plunging" bucker, who runs forward all the time while bucking; or he may buck steadily in one place, or "sun-fish,"—that is, bring first one shoulder down almost to the ground and then the other,— or else he may change ends while in the air. A first-class rider will sit throughout it all without moving from the saddle, quirting* his horse all the time, though his hat may be jarred off his head and his revolver out of its sheath. After a few jumps, however, the average man grasps hold of

* Quirt is the name of the short flexible riding-whip used throughout cowboy land. The term is a Spanish one.

the horn of the saddle—the delighted onlookers meanwhile earnestly advising him not to "go to leather"—and is contented to get through the affair in any shape provided he can escape without being thrown off. An accident is of necessity borne with a broad grin, as any attempt to resent the raillery of the bystanders—which is perfectly good-humored—would be apt to result disastrously. Cowboys are certainly extremely good riders. As a class they have no superiors. Of course, they would at first be at a disadvantage in steeple-chasing or fox-hunting, but their average of horsemanship is without doubt higher than that of the men who take part in these latter amusements. A cowboy would learn to ride across country in a quarter of the time it would take a cross-country rider to learn to handle a vicious bronco or to do good cow-work round and in a herd.

On such a day, when there is no regular work, there will often also be horse-races, as each outfit is pretty sure to have some running pony which it believes can outpace any other. These contests are always short-distance dashes, for but a few hundred yards. Horse-racing is a mania with most plainsmen, white or red. A man with a good racing pony will travel all about with it, often winning large sums, visiting alike cow ranches, frontier towns, and Indian encampments. Sometimes the race is "pony against pony," the victor taking both steeds. In racing the men ride bareback, as there are hardly any light saddles in the cow country. There will be intense excitement and very heavy betting over a race between two well-known horses, together with a good chance of blood being shed in the attendant quarrels. Indians and whites often race against each other as well as among themselves. I have seen several such contests, and in every case but one the white man happened to win. A race is usually run between two thick rows of spectators, on foot and on horseback, and as the racers pass, these rows close in behind them, every man yelling and shouting with all the strength of his lungs, and all waving their hats and cloaks to encourage the contestants, or firing off their revolvers and saddle guns. The little horses are fairly maddened, as is natural enough, and run as if they were crazy: were the distances longer some would be sure to drop in their tracks.

Besides the horse-races, which are, of course, the main attraction, the men at a round-up will often get up wrestling matches or foot-races. In fact, every one feels that he is off for a holiday; for after the monotony of a long winter, the cowboys look forward eagerly to the round-up, where the work is hard, it is true, but exciting and varied, and treated a good deal as a frolic. There is no eight-hour law in cowboy land: during round-up time we often count ourselves lucky if we get off with much less than sixteen hours; but the work is done in the saddle, and the men are spurred on all the time by the desire to outdo one another in feats of daring and skillful horsemanship. There is very little quarreling or fighting; and though the fun often takes the form of rather rough horse-play, yet the practice of carrying dangerous weapons makes cowboys show far more rough courtesy to each other and far less rudeness to strangers than is the case among, for instance, Eastern miners, or even lumbermen. When a quarrel may very probably result fatally, a man thinks twice before going into it:

TRAILING CATTLE.

warlike people or classes always treat one another with a certain amount of consideration and politeness. The moral tone of a cow-camp, indeed, is rather high than otherwise. Meanness, cowardice, and dishonesty are not tolerated. There is a high regard for truthfulness and keeping one's word, intense contempt for any kind of hypocrisy, and a hearty dislike for a man who shirks his work. Many of the men gamble and drink, but many do neither; and the conversation is not worse than in most bodies composed wholly of male human beings. A cowboy will not submit tamely to an insult, and is ever ready to avenge his own wrongs; nor has he an overwrought fear of shedding blood. He possesses, in fact, few of the emasculated, milk-and-water moralities admired by the pseudo-philanthropists; but he does possess, to a very high degree, the stern, manly qualities that are invaluable to a nation.

The method of work is simple. The mess-wagons and loose horses, after breaking camp in the morning, move on in a straight line for some few miles, going into camp again before midday; and the day herd, consisting of all the cattle that have been found far off their range, and which are to be brought back there, and of any others that it is necessary to gather, follows on afterwards. Meanwhile the cowboys scatter out and drive in all the cattle from the country round about, going perhaps ten or fifteen miles back from the line of march, and meeting at the place where camp has already been pitched. The wagons always keep some little distance from one another, and the saddle-bands do the same, so that the horses may not get mixed. It is rather picturesque to see the four-horse teams filing down at a trot through a pass among the buttes—the saddle-bands being driven along at a smart pace to one side or behind, the teamsters cracking their whips, and the horse-wranglers calling and shouting as they ride rapidly from side to side behind the horses, urging on the stragglers by dexterous touches with the knotted ends of their long lariats that are left trailing from the saddle. The country driven over is very rough, and it is often necessary to double up teams and put on eight horses to each wagon in going up an unusually steep pitch, or hauling through a deep mud-hole, or over a river crossing where there is quicksand.

The speed and thoroughness with which a country can be worked depends, of course, very largely upon the number of riders. Ours is probably about an average round-up as regards size. The last spring I was out, there were half a dozen wagons along; the saddle-bands numbered about a hundred each; and the morning we started, sixty men in the saddle splashed across the shallow ford of the river that divided the plain where we had camped from the valley of the long winding creek up which we were first to work.

In the morning the cook is preparing breakfast long before the first glimmer of dawn. As soon as it is ready, probably about 3 o'clock, he utters a long-drawn shout, and all the sleepers feel it is time to be up on the instant, for they know there can be no such thing as delay on the round-up, under penalty of being set afoot. Accordingly, they bundle out, rubbing their eyes and yawning, draw on their boots and trousers,—if they have taken the latter off,—roll up and cord their bedding, and usually without any attempt at washing crowd over to the little smoldering fire, which is placed in a hole dug in the ground, so that there may be no risk of its spreading. The men are rarely very hungry at breakfast, and it is a meal that has to be eaten in shortest order, so it is perhaps the least important. Each man, as he comes up, grasps a tin cup and plate from the mess-box, pours out his tea or coffee, with sugar, but, of course, no milk, helps himself to one or two of the biscuits that have been baked in a Dutch oven, and perhaps also to a slice of the fat pork swimming in the grease of the frying-pan, ladles himself out some beans, if there are any, and squats down on the ground to eat his breakfast. The meal is not an elaborate one; nevertheless a man will have to hurry if he wishes to eat it before hearing the foreman sing out, "Come, boys, catch your horses"; when he must drop everything and run out to the wagon with his lariat. The night wrangler is now bringing in the saddle-band, which he has been up all night guarding. A rope corral is rigged up by stretching a rope from each wheel of one side of the wagon, making a V-shaped space, into which the saddle-horses are driven. Certain men stand around to keep them inside, while the others catch the horses: many outfits have one man to do all the roping. As soon as each has caught his horse—usually a strong, tough animal, the small, quick ponies being reserved for the work round the herd in the afternoon—the band, now in charge of the day wrangler, is turned loose, and every one saddles up as fast as possible. It still lacks some time of being sunrise, and the air has in it the peculiar chill of the early morning. When all are saddled, many of the horses bucking and dancing about, the riders from the different wagons all assemble at the one where the captain is sitting, already mounted. He waits a very short time—for laggards receive but scant mercy—before announcing the proposed camping-place and parceling out the work among those present. If, as is usually the case, the line of march is along a river or creek, he appoints some man to take a dozen others and drive down (or up) it ahead of the day herd, so that the latter will not have to travel through other cattle; the day herd itself being driven and guarded by a dozen men detached for that purpose. The rest of the riders are divided into two bands, placed under men who know the country, and start out, one on each side, to bring in every head for fifteen miles back. The captain then himself rides down to the new camping-place, so as to be there as soon as any cattle are brought in.

Meanwhile the two bands, a score of riders in each, separate and make their way in opposite directions. The leader of each tries to get such a "scatter" on his men that they will cover completely all the land gone over. This morning work is called circle riding, and is peculiarly hard in the Bad Lands on account of the remarkably broken, rugged nature of the country. The men come in on lines that tend to a common center— as if the sticks of a fan were curved. As the band goes out, the leader

THE ROPE CORRAL.

from time to time detaches one or two men to ride down through certain sections of the country, making the shorter, or what are called inside, circles, while he keeps on; and finally, retaining as companions the two or three whose horses are toughest, makes the longest or outside circle himself, going clear back to the divide, or whatever the point may be that marks the limit of the round-up work, and then turning and working straight to the meeting-place. Each man, of course, brings in every head of cattle he can see.

These long, swift rides in the glorious spring mornings are not soon to be forgotten. The sweet, fresh air, with a touch of sharpness thus early in the day, and the rapid motion of the fiery little horse combine to make a man's blood thrill and leap with sheer buoyant light-heartedness and eager, exultant pleasure in the boldness and freedom of the life he is leading. As we climb the steep sides of the first range of buttes, wisps of wavering mist still cling in the hollows of the valley; when we come out on the top of the first great plateau, the sun flames up over its edge, and in the level, red beams the galloping horsemen throw long fantastic shadows. Black care rarely sits behind a rider whose pace is fast enough; at any rate, not when he first feels the horse move under him.

Sometimes we trot or pace, and again we lope or gallop; the few who are to take the outside circle must needs ride both hard and fast. Although only grass-fed, the horses are tough and wiry; and, moreover, are each used but once in four days, or thereabouts, so they stand the work well. The course out lies across great grassy plateaus, along knife-like ridge crests, among winding valleys and ravines, and over acres of barren, sun-scorched buttes, that look grimly grotesque and forbidding, while in the Bad Lands the riders unhesitatingly go down and over places where it seems impossible that a horse should even stand. The line of horsemen will quarter down the side of a butte, where every pony has to drop from ledge to ledge like a goat, and will go over the shoulder of a soapstone cliff, when wet and slippery, with a series of plunges and scrambles which if unsuccessful would land horses and riders in the bottom of the cañon-like washout below. In descending a clay butte after a rain, the pony will put all four feet together and slide down to the bottom almost or quite on his haunches. In very wet weather the Bad Lands are absolutely impassable; but if the ground is not slippery, it is a remarkable place that can shake the matter-of-course confidence felt by the rider in the capacity of his steed to go anywhere.

When the men on the outside circle have reached the bound set them,—whether it is a low divide, a group of jagged hills, the edge of the rolling, limitless prairie, or the long, waste reaches of alkali and sage brush,—they turn their horses' heads and begin to work down the branches of the creeks, one or two riding down the bottom, while the others keep off to the right and the left, a little ahead and fairly high up on the side hills, so as to command as much of a view as possible. On the level or rolling prairies the cattle can be seen a long way off, and it is an easy matter to gather and to drive them; but in the Bad Lands every little pocket, basin, and coulée has to be searched, every gorge or ravine entered, and the dense patches of brushwood and spindling, wind-beaten trees closely examined. All the cattle are carried on ahead down the creek; and it is curious to watch the different behavior of the different breeds. A cowboy riding off to one side of the creek, and seeing a number of long-horned Texans grazing in the branches of a set of coulées, has merely to ride across the upper ends of these, uttering the drawn-out "ei-koh-h-h," so familiar to the cattle-men, and the long-horns will stop grazing, stare fixedly at him, and then, wheeling, strike off down the coulées at a trot, tails in air, to be carried along by the center riders when they reach the main creek into which the coulées lead. Our own range cattle are not so wild, but nevertheless are easy to drive; while Eastern-raised beasts have little fear of a horseman, and merely stare stupidly at him until he rides directly towards them. Every little bunch of stock is thus collected, and all are driven along together. At the place where some large fork joins the main creek another band may be met, driven by some of the men who have left earlier in the day to take one of the shorter circles; and thus, before coming down to the bottom where the wagons are camped and where the actual "round-up" itself is to take place, this one herd may include a couple of thousand head; or, on the other hand, the longest ride may not result in the finding of a dozen animals. As soon as the riders are in, they disperse to their respective wagons to get dinner and change horses, leaving the cattle to be held by one or two of their number. If only a small number of cattle have been gathered, they will all be run into one herd; if there are many of them, however, the different herds will be held separate.

A plain where a round-up is taking place offers a picturesque sight. I well remember one such. It was on a level bottom in a bend of the river, which here made an almost semicircular sweep. The bottom was in shape a long oval, hemmed in by an unbroken line of steep bluffs so that it looked like an amphitheater. Across the faces of the dazzling white cliffs there were sharp bands of black and red, drawn by the coal seams and the layers of burned clay: the leaves of the trees and the grass had the vivid green of spring-time. The wagons were camped among the cottonwood trees fringing the river, a thin column of smoke rising up from beside each. The horses were grazing round the outskirts, those of each wagon by themselves and kept from going too near the others by their watchful guard. In the great circular corral, towards one end, the men were already branding calves, while the whole middle of the bottom was covered with lowing herds of cattle and shouting, galloping cowboys. Apparently there was nothing but dust, noise, and confusion; but in reality the work was proceeding all the while with the utmost rapidity and certainty.

As soon as, or even before, the last circle riders have come in and have snatched a few hasty mouthfuls to serve as their midday meal, we begin to work the herd—or herds, if the one herd would be of too unwieldy size. The animals are held in a compact bunch, most of the riders forming a ring outside, while a couple from each ranch successively look the herds through and cut out those marked with their own brand. It is difficult, in such a mass of moving beasts,—for they do not stay still, but keep weaving in and out among each other,—to find all of one's own animals: a man must have natural gifts, as well as great experience, before he becomes a good brand-reader and is able really to "clean up a herd"—that is, be sure he has left nothing of his own in it.

CUTTING OUT A STEER.

To do good work in cutting out from a herd, not only should the rider be a good horseman, but he should also have a skillful, thoroughly trained horse. A good cutting pony is not common, and is generally too valuable to be used anywhere but in the herd. Such an one enters thoroughly into the spirit of the thing, and finds out immediately the animal his master is after; he will then follow it closely of his own accord through every wheel and double at top speed. When looking through the herd, it is necessary to move slowly; and when any animal is found it is taken to the outskirts at a walk, so as not to alarm the others. Once at the outside, however, the cowboy has to ride like lightning; for as soon as the beast he is after finds itself separated from its companions it endeavors to break back among them, and a young, range-raised steer or heifer runs like a deer. In cutting out a cow and a calf two men have to work together. As the animals of a brand are cut out they are received and held apart by some rider detailed for the purpose, who is said to be "holding the cut."

All this time the men holding the herd have their hands full, for some animal is continually trying to break out, when the nearest man flies at it at once and after a smart chase brings it back to its fellows. As soon as all the cows, calves, and whatever else is being gathered have been cut out, the rest are driven clear off the ground and turned loose, being headed in the direction contrary to that in which we travel the following day. Then the riders surround the next herd, the men holding cuts move them up near it, and the work is begun anew.

If it is necessary to throw an animal, either to examine a brand or for any other reason, half a dozen men will have their ropes down at once; and then it is spur and quirt in the rivalry to see which can outdo the other until the beast is roped and thrown. A first-class hand will, unaided, rope, throw, and tie down a cow or steer in wonderfully short time; one of the favorite tests of competitive skill among the cowboys is the speed with which this feat can be accomplished. Usually, however, one man ropes the animal by the head and another at the same time gets the loop of his lariat over one or both its hind legs, when it is twisted over and stretched out in a second. In following an animal on horseback the man keeps steadily swinging the rope round his head, by a dexterous motion of the wrist only, until he gets a chance to throw it; when on foot, especially if catching horses in a corral, the loop is allowed to drag loosely on the ground. A good roper will hurl out the coil with marvelous accuracy and force; it fairly whistles through the air, and settles round the object with almost infallible certainty. Mexicans make the best ropers; but some Texans are very little behind them. A good horse takes as much interest in the work as does his rider, and the instant the noose settles over the victim wheels and braces himself to meet the shock, standing with his legs firmly planted, the steer or cow being thrown with a jerk. An unskillful rider and untrained horse will often themselves be thrown when the strain comes.

Sometimes an animal—usually a cow or steer, but, strangely enough, very rarely a bull—will get fighting mad, and turn on the men. If on the drive, such a beast usually is simply dropped out; but if they have time, nothing delights the cowboys more than an encounter of this sort, and the charging brute is roped and tied down in short order. Often such an one will make a very vicious fight, and is most dangerous. Once a fighting cow kept several of us busy for nearly an hour; she gored two ponies, one of them, which was, luckily, hurt but slightly, being my own pet cutting horse. If a steer is hauled out of a mud-hole, its first act is usually to charge the rescuer.

As soon as all the brands of cattle are worked, and the animals that are to be driven along have been put in the day herd, attention is turned to the cows and calves, which are already gathered in different bands, consisting each of all the cows of a certain brand and all the calves that are following them. If there is a corral, each band is in turn driven into it; if there is none, a ring of riders does duty in its place. A fire is

BRANDING A CALF.

built, the irons heated, and a dozen men dismount to, as it is called, "wrestle" the calves. The best two ropers go in on their horses to catch the latter; one man keeps tally, a couple put on the brands, and the others seize, throw, and hold the little unfortunates. A first-class roper invariably catches the calf by both hind feet, and then, having taken a twist with his lariat round the horn of the saddle, drags the bawling little creature, extended at full-length, up to the fire, where it is held before it can make a struggle.   A less skillful roper catches round the neck, and then, if the calf is a large one, the man who seizes it has his hands full, as the bleating, bucking animal develops astonishing strength, cuts the wildest capers,

BRANDING A HORSE.

and resists frantically and with all its power.   If there are seventy or eighty calves in a corral, the scene is one of the greatest confusion.   The ropers, spurring and checking the fierce little horses, drag the calves up so quickly that a dozen men can hardly hold them ; the men with the irons, blackened with soot, run to and fro ; the calf-wrestlers, grimy with blood, dust, and sweat, work like beavers ; while with the voice of a stentor the tally-man shouts out the number and sex of each calf.   The dust rises in clouds, and the shouts, cheers, curses, and laughter of the men unite with the lowing of the cows and the frantic bleating of the roped calves to make a perfect babel.   Now and then an old cow turns vicious and puts every one out of the corral.   Or a *maverick* bull,—that is, an unbranded bull,—a yearling or a two-years-old, is caught, thrown, and branded ; when he is let up there is sure to be a fine scatter.   Down goes his head, and he bolts at the nearest man, who makes out of the way at top speed, amidst roars of laughter from all of his companions ; while the men holding down calves swear savagely as they dodge charging mavericks, trampling horses, and taut lariats with frantic, plunging little beasts at the farther ends.

Every morning certain riders are detached to drive and to guard the day herd, which is most monotonous work, the men being on from 4 in the morning till 8 in the evening, the only rest coming at dinner-time, when they change horses. When the herd has reached the camping-ground there is nothing to do but to loll listlessly over the saddle-bow in the blazing sun watching the cattle feed and sleep, and seeing that they do not spread out too much. Plodding slowly along on the trail through the columns of dust stirred up by the hoofs is not much better. Cattle travel best and fastest strung out in long lines; the swiftest taking the lead in single file, while the weak and the lazy, the young calves and the poor cows, crowd together in the rear. Two men travel along with the leaders, one on each side, to point them in the right direction; one or two others keep by the flanks, and the rest are in the rear to act as "drag-drivers" and hurry up the phalanx of reluctant weaklings. If the foremost of the string travels too fast, one rider will go along on the trail a few rods ahead, and thus keep them back so that those in the rear will not be left behind.

Generally all this is very tame and irksome; but by fits and starts there will be little flurries of excitement. Two or three of the circle riders may unexpectedly come over a butte near by with a bunch of cattle, which at once start for the day herd, and then there will be a few minutes' furious riding hither and thither to keep them out. Or the cattle may begin to run, and then get "milling"—that is, all crowd together into a mass like a ball, wherein they move round and round, trying to keep their heads towards the center, and refusing to leave it. The only way to start them is to force one's horse in among them and cut out some of their number, which then begin to travel off by themselves, when the others will probably follow. But in spite of occasional incidents of this kind, day-herding has a dreary sameness about it that makes the men dislike and seek to avoid it.

From 8 in the evening till 4 in the morning the day herd becomes a night herd. Each wagon in succession undertakes to guard it for a night, dividing the time into watches of two hours apiece, a couple of riders taking each watch. This is generally chilly and tedious; but at times it is accompanied by intense excitement and danger, when the cattle become stampeded, whether by storm or otherwise. The first and the last watches are those chosen by preference; the others are disagreeable, the men having to turn out cold and sleepy, in the pitchy darkness, the two hours of chilly wakefulness completely breaking the night's rest. The first guards have to bed the cattle down, though the day-herders often do this themselves: it simply consists in hemming them into as small a space as pos-

THE HERD AT NIGHT.

sible, and then riding round them until they lie down and fall asleep.
Often, especially at first, this takes some time—the beasts will keep rising
and lying down again. When at last most become quiet, some perverse
brute of a steer will deliberately hook them all up; they keep moving in
and out among one another, and long strings of animals suddenly start out
from the herd at a stretching walk, and are turned back by the nearest

cowboy only to break forth at a new spot. When finally they have lain down and are chewing their cud or slumbering, the two night guards begin riding round them in opposite ways, often, on very dark nights, calling or singing to them, as the sound of the human voice on such occasions seems to have a tendency to quiet them. In inky black weather, especially when rainy, it is both difficult and unpleasant work; the main trust must be placed in the horse, which, if old at the business, will of its own accord keep pacing steadily round the herd, and head off any animals that, unseen by the rider's eyes in the darkness, are trying to break out. Usually the watch passes off without incident, but on rare occasions the cattle become restless and prone to stampede. Anything may then start them —the plunge of a horse, the sudden approach of a coyote, or the arrival of some outside steers or cows that have smelt them and come up. Every animal in the herd will be on its feet in an instant, as if by an electric shock, and off with a rush, horns and tail up. Then, no matter how rough the ground nor how pitchy black the night, the cowboys must ride for all there is in them and spare neither their own nor their horses' necks. Perhaps their charges break away and are lost altogether; perhaps, by desperate galloping, they may head them off, get them running in a circle, and finally stop them. Once stopped, they may break again, and possibly divide up, one cowboy, perhaps, following each band. I have known six such stops and renewed stampedes to take place in one night, the cowboy staying with his ever-diminishing herd of steers until daybreak, when he managed to get them under control again, and, by careful humoring of his jaded, staggering horse, finally brought those that were left back to the camp, several miles distant. The riding in these night stampedes is wild and dangerous to a degree, especially if the man gets caught in the rush of the beasts. It also frequently necessitates an immense amount of work in collecting the scattered animals. On one such occasion a small party of us were thirty-six hours in the saddle, dismounting only to change horses or to eat. We were almost worn out at the end of the time; but it must be kept in mind that for a long spell of such work a stock-saddle is far less tiring than the ordinary Eastern or English one, and in every way superior to it.

By very hard riding, such a stampede may sometimes be prevented. Once we were bringing a thousand head of young cattle down to my lower ranch, and as the river was high were obliged to take the inland trail. The third night we were forced to make a dry camp, the cattle having had no water since the morning. Nevertheless, we got them bedded down without difficulty, and one of the cowboys and myself stood first guard. But very soon after nightfall, when the darkness had become complete, the thirsty brutes of one accord got on their feet and tried to break out.   The only salvation was to keep them close together, as, if they once got scattered, we knew they could never be gathered; so I kept on one side, and the cowboy on the other, and never in my life did I ride so hard. In the darkness I could but dimly see the shadowy outlines of the herd, as with whip and spurs I ran the pony along its edge, turning back the beasts at one point barely in time to wheel and keep them in at another.   The ground was cut up by numerous little gullies, and each of us got several falls, horses and riders turning complete somersaults. We were dripping with sweat, and our ponies quivering and trembling like quaking aspens, when, after more than an hour of the most violent exertion, we finally got the herd quieted again.

On another occasion while with the round-up we were spared an excessively unpleasant night only because there happened to be two or three great corrals not more than a mile or so away.   All day long it had been raining heavily, and we were well drenched; but towards evening it lulled a little, and the day herd, a very large one, of some two thousand head, was gathered on an open bottom.   We had turned the horses loose, and in our oilskin slickers cowered, soaked and comfortless, under the lee of the wagon, to take a meal of damp bread and lukewarm tea, the sizzling embers of the fire having about given up the ghost after a fruitless struggle with the steady downpour.   Suddenly the wind began to come in quick, sharp gusts, and soon a regular blizzard was blowing, driving the rain in stinging level sheets before it.   Just as we were preparing to turn into bed, with the certainty of a night of more or less chilly misery ahead of us, one of my men, an iron-faced personage, whom no one would ever have dreamed had a weakness for poetry, looked towards the plain where the cattle were, and remarked, "I guess there's 'racing and chasing on Cannobie Lea' now, sure." Following his gaze, I saw that the cattle had begun to drift before the storm, the night guards being evidently unable to cope with them, while at the other wagons riders were saddling in hot haste and spurring off to their help through the blinding rain.   Some of us at once ran out to our own saddle-band. All of the ponies were standing huddled together, with their heads down and their tails to the wind.   They were wild and restive enough usually; but the storm had cowed them, and we were able to catch them without either rope or halter.   We made quick work of saddling; and the second each man was ready, away he loped through the dusk, splashing and slipping in the pools of water that studded the muddy plain.   Most of the

IN A STAMPEDE.

riders were already out when we arrived.   The cattle were gathered in a
compact, wedge-shaped, or rather fan-shaped mass, with their tails to the
wind—that is, towards the thin end of the wedge or fan.   In front of this
fan-shaped mass of frightened, maddened beasts was a long line of cow-

boys, each muffled in his slicker and with his broad hat pulled down over his eyes, to shield him from the pelting rain. When the cattle were quiet for a moment every horseman at once turned round with his back to the wind, and the whole line stood as motionless as so many sentries. Then, if the cattle began to spread out and overlap at the ends, or made a rush and broke through at one part of the lines, there would be a change into wild activity. The men, shouting and swaying in their saddles, darted to and fro with reckless speed, utterly heedless of danger—now racing to the threatened point, now checking and wheeling their horses so sharply as to bring them square on their haunches, or even throw them flat down, while the hoofs plowed long furrows in the slippery soil, until, after some minutes of this mad galloping hither and thither, the herd, having drifted a hundred yards or so, would be once more brought up standing. We always had to let them drift a little to prevent their spreading out too much. The din of the thunder was terrific, peal following peal until they mingled in one continuous, rumbling roar; and at every thunder-clap louder than its fellows the cattle would try to break away. Darkness had set in, but each flash of lightning showed us a dense array of tossing horns and staring eyes. It grew always harder to hold in the herd; but the drift took us along to the corrals already spoken of, whose entrances were luckily to windward. As soon as we reached the first we cut off part of the herd, and turned it within; and after again doing this with the second, we were able to put all the remaining animals into the third. The instant the cattle were housed five-sixths of the horsemen started back at full speed for the wagons; the rest of us barely waited to put up the bars and make the corrals secure before galloping after them. We had to ride right in the teeth of the driving storm; and once at the wagons we made small delay in crawling under our blankets, damp though the latter were, for we were ourselves far too wet, stiff, and cold not to hail with grateful welcome any kind of shelter from the wind and the rain.

All animals were benumbed by the violence of this gale of cold rain: a prairie chicken rose from under my horse's feet so heavily that, thoughtlessly striking at it, I cut it down with my whip; while when a jack rabbit got up ahead of us, it was barely able to limp clumsily out of our way.

But though there is much work and hardship, rough fare, monotony, and exposure connected with the round-up, yet there are few men who do not look forward to it and back to it with pleasure. The only fault to be found is that the hours of work are so long that one does not usually have enough time to sleep. The food, if rough, is good: beef, bread, pork, beans, coffee or tea, always canned tomatoes, and often rice, canned corn, or sauce made from dried apples. The men are good-humored, bold, and thoroughly interested in their business, continually vying with one another in the effort to see which can do the work best. It is superbly health-giving, and is full of excitement and adventure, calling for the exhibition of pluck, self-reliance, hardihood, and dashing horsemanship; and of all forms of physical labor the easiest and pleasantest is to sit in the saddle.

ROPED!

A TEXAN PONY.

WINTER WEATHER

LINE RIDING IN WINTER.

V

Winter Weather

WHEN the days have dwindled to their shortest, and the nights seem never ending, then all the great northern plains are changed into an abode of iron desolation. Sometimes furious gales blow out of the north, driving before them the clouds of blinding snow-dust, wrapping the mantle of death round every unsheltered being that faces their unshackled anger. They roar in a thunderous bass as they sweep across the prairie or whirl through the naked cañons; they shiver the great brittle cotton-woods, and beneath their rough touch the icy limbs of the pines that cluster in the gorges sing like the chords of an Æolian harp. Again, in the coldest midwinter weather, not a breath of wind may stir; and then the still, merciless, terrible cold that broods over the earth like the shadow of silent death seems even more dreadful in its gloomy rigor than is the lawless madness of the storms. All the land is like granite; the great rivers stand still in their beds, as if turned to frosted steel. In the long nights there is no sound to break the lifeless silence. Under the ceaseless, shifting play of the Northern Lights, or lighted only by the wintry brilliance of the stars, the snow-clad plains stretch out into dead and endless wastes of glimmering white.

Then the great fire-place of the ranch house is choked with blazing logs, and at night we have to sleep under so many blankets that the weight is fairly oppressive. Outside, the shaggy ponies huddle together in the corral, while long icicles hang from their lips, and the hoar-frost whitens the hollow backs of the cattle. For the ranchman the winter is occasionally a pleasant holiday, but more often an irksome period of enforced rest and gloomy foreboding.

In the winter there is much less work than at any other season, but what there is involves great hardship and exposure. Many of the men are discharged after the summer is over, and during much of the cold weather there is little to do except hunt now and then, and in very bitter days lounge listlessly about the house. But some of the men are out in the line camps, and the ranchman has occasionally to make the round of these; and besides that, one or more of the cowboys who are at home ought to be out every day when the cattle have become weak, so as to pick up and drive in any beast that will otherwise evidently fail to get through the season—a cow that has had an unusually early calf being particularly apt to need attention. The horses shift for themselves and need no help. Often, in winter, the Indians cut down the cottonwood trees and feed the tops to their ponies; but this is not done to keep them from starving, but only to keep them from wandering off in search of grass. Besides, the ponies are very fond of the bark of the young cottonwood shoots, and it is healthy for them.

The men in the line camps lead a hard life, for they have to be out in every kind of weather, and should be especially active and watchful during the storms. The camps are established along some line which it is proposed to make the boundary of the cattle's drift in a given direction. For example, we care very little whether our cattle wander to the Yellowstone; but we strongly object to their drifting east and south-east towards the granger country and the Sioux reservation, especially as when they drift that way they come out on flat, bare plains where there is danger of perishing. Accordingly, the cowmen along the Little Missouri have united in establishing a row of camps to the east of the river, along the line where the broken ground meets the prairie. The camps are usually for two men each, and some fifteen or twenty miles apart; then, in the morning, its two men start out in opposite ways, each riding till he meets his neighbor of the next camp nearest on that side, when he returns. The camp itself is sometimes merely a tent pitched in a sheltered coulée, but ought to be either made of logs or else a dug-out in the ground. A small corral and horse-shed is near by, with enough hay for the ponies, of which each rider has two or three. In riding over the beat each man drives any cattle that have come near it back into the Bad Lands, and if he sees by the hoof-marks that a few have strayed out over the line very recently, he will follow and fetch them home. They must be shoved well back into the Bad Lands before a great storm strikes them; for if they once begin to drift in masses before an icy gale it is impossible for a small number of men to hold them, and the only thing is to let them go, and then to organize an expedition to follow them as soon as possible.   Line riding is very cold work, and dangerous too, when the men have to be out in a blinding snow-storm, or in a savage blizzard that takes the spirit in the thermometer far down below zero.   In the worst storms it is impossible for any man to be out.

But other kinds of work besides line riding necessitate exposure to bitter weather.   Once, while spending a few days over on Beaver Creek hunting up a lost horse, I happened to meet a cowboy who was out on the same errand, and made friends with him.   We started home together across the open prairies, but were caught in a very heavy snow-storm almost immediately after leaving the ranch where we had spent the night. We were soon completely turned round, the great soft flakes—for, luckily, it was not cold—almost blinding us, and we had to travel entirely by compass.   After feeling our way along for eight or nine hours, we finally got down into the broken country near Sentinel Butte and came across an empty hut, a welcome sight to men as cold, hungry, and tired as we were.   In this hut we passed the night very comfortably, picketing our horses in a sheltered nook near by, with plenty of hay from an old stack. To while away the long evening, I read Hamlet aloud, from a little pocket Shakspere.   The cowboy, a Texan,—one of the best riders I have seen, and also a very intelligent as well as a thoroughly good fellow in every way,—was greatly interested in it and commented most shrewdly on the parts he liked, especially Polonius's advice to Laertes, which he translated into more homely language with great relish, and ended with the just criticism that "old Shakspere saveyed human natur' some"— savey being a verb presumably adapted into the limited plains' vocabulary from the Spanish.

Even for those who do not have to look up stray horses, and who are not forced to ride the line day in and day out, there is apt to be some hardship and danger in being abroad during the bitter weather; yet a ride in midwinter is certainly fascinating.   The great white country wrapped in the powdery snow-drift seems like another land; and the familiar landmarks are so changed that a man must be careful lest he lose his way, for the discomfort of a night in the open during such weather is very great indeed.   When the sun is out the glare from the endless white stretches dazzles the eyes; and if the gray snow-clouds hang low and only let a pale, wan light struggle through, the lonely wastes become fairly appalling in their desolation.   For hour after hour a man may go on and see no sign of life except, perhaps, a big white owl sweeping noiselessly by, so that in the dark it looks like a snow-wreath; the cold gradually chilling the rider to the bones, as he draws his fur cap tight over his ears and muffles his face in the huge collar of his wolf-skin coat, and making the shaggy little steed drop head and tail as it picks its way over the frozen soil.   There are few moments more pleasant than the home-coming, when, in the gathering darkness, after crossing the last chain of ice-covered buttes, or after coming round the last turn in the wind-swept valley, we see, through the leafless trees, or across the frozen river, the red gleam of the firelight as it shines through the ranch windows and flickers over the trunks of the cottonwoods outside, warming a man's blood by the mere hint of the warmth awaiting him within.

The winter scenery is especially striking in the Bad Lands, with their queer fantastic formations.   Among the most interesting features are the burning mines.   These are formed by the coal seams that get on fire. They vary greatly in size.   Some send up smoke-columns that are visible miles away, while others are not noticeable a few rods off.   The old ones gradually burn away, while new ones unexpectedly break out.   Thus, last fall, one suddenly appeared but half a mile from the ranch house.   We never knew it was there until one cold moonlight night, when we were riding home, we rounded the corner of a ravine and saw in our path a tall white column of smoke rising from a rift in the snowy crags ahead of us. As the trail was over perfectly familiar ground, we were for a moment almost as startled as if we had seen a ghost.

The burning mines are uncanny places, anyhow.   A strong smell of sulphur hangs round them, the heated earth crumbles and cracks, and through the long clefts that form in it we can see the lurid glow of the subterranean fires, with here and there tongues of blue or cherry colored flame dancing up to the surface.

The winters vary greatly in severity with us.   During some seasons men can go lightly clad even in January and February, and the cattle hardly suffer at all; during others there will be spells of bitter weather, accompanied by furious blizzards, which render it impossible for days and weeks at a time for men to stir out-of-doors at all, save at the risk of their lives.   Then line rider, ranchman, hunter, and teamster alike all have to keep within doors.   I have known of several cases of men freezing to death when caught in shelterless places by such a blizzard, a strange fact being that in about half of them the doomed man had evidently gone mad before dying, and had stripped himself of most of his clothes, the body when found being nearly naked.   On our ranch we have never had any bad accidents, although every winter some of us get more or less frost-bitten.   My last experience in this line was while returning

CATTLE DRIFTING BEFORE THE STORM.

by moonlight from a successful hunt after mountain sheep. The thermometer was 26° below zero, and we had had no food for twelve hours. I became numbed, and before I was aware of it had frozen my face, one foot, both knees, and one hand. Luckily, I reached the ranch before serious damage was done.

About once every six or seven years we have a season when these storms follow one another almost without interval throughout the winter months, and then the loss among the stock is frightful. One such winter occurred in 1880–81. This was when there were very few ranchmen in the country. The grass was so good that the old range stock escaped pretty well; but the trail herds were almost destroyed. The next severe winter was that of 1886–87, when the rush of incoming herds had overstocked the ranges, and the loss was in consequence fairly appalling, especially to the outfits that had just put on cattle.

The snow-fall was unprecedented, both for its depth and for the way it lasted; and it was this, and not the cold, that caused the loss. About the

13

middle of November the storms began. Day after day the snow came
down, thawing and then freezing and piling itself higher and higher. By
January the drifts had filled the ravines and coulées almost level. The snow
lay in great masses on the plateaus and river bottoms; and this lasted
until the end of February. The preceding summer we had been visited by
a prolonged drought, so that the short, scanty grass was already well
cropped down; the snow covered what pasturage there was to the depth
of several feet, and the cattle could not get at it at all, and could hardly
move round. It was all but impossible to travel on horseback—except
on a few well-beaten trails. It was dangerous to attempt to penetrate the
Bad Lands, whose shape had been completely altered by the great white
mounds and drifts. The starving cattle died by scores of thousands
before their helpless owners' eyes. The bulls, the cows who were suck-
ling calves, or who were heavy with calf, the weak cattle that had just been
driven up on the trail, and the late calves suffered most; the old range
animals did better, and the steers best of all; but the best was bad
enough. Even many of the horses died. An outfit near me lost half its
saddle-band, the animals having been worked so hard that they were very
thin when fall came.

In the thick brush the stock got some shelter and sustenance. They
gnawed every twig and bough they could get at. They browsed the bitter
sage brush down to where the branches were the thickness of a man's
finger. When near a ranch they crowded into the outhouses and sheds
to die, and fences had to be built around the windows to keep the wild-
eyed, desperate beasts from thrusting their heads through the glass panes.
In most cases it was impossible either to drive them to the haystacks or to
haul the hay out to them. The deer even were so weak as to be easily run
down; and on one or two of the plateaus where there were bands of
antelope, these wary creatures grew so numbed and feeble that they could
have been slaughtered like rabbits. But the hunters could hardly get out,
and could bring home neither hide nor meat, so the game went unharmed.

The way in which the cattle got through the winter depended largely
on the different localities in which the bands were caught when the first
heavy snows came. A group of animals in a bare valley, without underbrush and with steepish sides, would all die, weak and strong alike; they
could get no food and no shelter, and so there would not be a hoof left.
On the other hand, hundreds wintered on the great thickly wooded bottoms near my ranch house with little more than ordinary loss, though a
skinny sorry-looking crew by the time the snow melted. In intermediate
places the strong survived and the weak perished.

It would be impossible to imagine any sight more dreary and melancholy than that offered by the ranges when the snow went off in March. The land was a mere barren waste; not a green thing could be seen; the dead grass eaten off till the country looked as if it had been shaved with a razor. Occasionally among the desolate hills a rider would come across a band of gaunt, hollow-flanked cattle feebly cropping the sparse, dry pasturage, too listless to move out of the way; and the blackened carcasses lay in the sheltered spots, some stretched out, others in as natural a position as if the animals had merely lain down to rest. It was small wonder that cheerful stockmen were rare objects that spring.

Our only comfort was that we did not, as usual, suffer a heavy loss from weak cattle getting mired down in the springs and mud-holes when the ice broke up—for all the weak animals were dead already. The truth is, ours is a primitive industry, and we suffer the reverses as well as enjoy the successes only known to primitive peoples. A hard winter is to us in the north what a dry summer is to Texas or Australia—what seasons of famine once were to all peoples. We still live in an iron age that the old civilized world has long passed by. The men of the border reckon upon stern and unending struggles with their iron-bound surroundings; against the grim harshness of their existence they set the strength and the abounding vitality that come with it. They run risks to life and limb that are unknown to the dwellers in cities; and what the men freely brave, the beasts that they own must also sometimes suffer.

HORSE OF THE CANADIAN NORTH-WEST.

FRONTIER TYPES

THE FUGITIVE.

VI

Frontier Types

A MEXICAN VAQUERO.

THE old race of Rocky Mountain hunters and trappers, of reckless, dauntless Indian fighters, is now fast dying out. Yet here and there these restless wanderers of the untrodden wilderness still linger, in wooded fastnesses so inaccessible that the miners have not yet explored them, in mountain valleys so far off that no ranchman has yet driven his herds thither. To this day many of them wear the fringed tunic or hunting-shirt, made of buckskin or homespun, and belted in at the waist,—the most picturesque and distinctively national dress ever worn in America. It was the dress in which Daniel Boone was clad when he first passed through the trackless forests of the Alleghanies and penetrated into the heart of Kentucky, to enjoy such hunting as no man of his race had ever had before; it was the dress worn by grim old Davy Crockett when he fell at the Alamo. The wild soldiery of the backwoods wore it when they marched to victory over Ferguson and Pakenham, at King's Mountain and New Orleans; when they conquered the French towns of the Illinois; and when they won at the cost of Red Eagle's warriors the bloody triumph of the Horseshoe Bend.

These old-time hunters have been the forerunners of the white advance throughout all our Western land. Soon after the beginning of the present century they boldly struck out beyond the Mississippi, steered their way across the flat and endless seas of grass, or pushed up the valleys of the great lonely rivers, crossed the passes that wound among the towering peaks of the Rockies, toiled over the melancholy wastes of sage brush and alkali, and at last, breaking through the gloomy woodland that belts the coast, they looked out on the heaving waves of the greatest of all the oceans. They lived for months, often for years, among the Indians, now as friends, now as foes, warring, hunting, and marrying with them; they acted as guides for exploring parties, as scouts for the soldiers who from time to time were sent against the different hostile tribes. At long intervals they came into some frontier settlement or some fur company's fort, posted in the heart of the wilderness, to dispose of their bales of furs, or to replenish their stock of ammunition and purchase a scanty supply of coarse food and clothing.

From that day to this they have not changed their way of life. But there are not many of them left now. The basin of the Upper Missouri was their last stronghold, being the last great hunting-ground of the Indians, with whom the white trappers were always fighting and bickering, but who nevertheless by their presence protected the game that gave the trappers their livelihood. My cattle were among the very first to come into the land, at a time when the buffalo and beaver still abounded, and then the old hunters were common. Many a time I have hunted with them, spent the night in their smoky cabins, or had them as guests at my ranch. But in a couple of years after the inrush of the cattle-men the last herds of the buffalo were destroyed, and the beaver were trapped out of all the plains' streams. Then the hunters vanished likewise, save that here and there one or two still remain in some nook or out-of-the-way corner. The others wandered off restlessly over the land,—some to join their brethren in the Cœur d'Alêne or the northern Rockies, others to the coast ranges or to far-away Alaska. Moreover, their ranks were soon thinned by death, and the places of the dead were no longer taken by new recruits. They led hard lives, and the unending strain of their toilsome and dangerous existence shattered even such iron frames as theirs. They were killed in drunken brawls, or in nameless fights with roving Indians; they died by one of the thousand accidents incident to the business of their lives,—by flood or quicksand, by cold or starvation, by the stumble of a horse or a footslip on the edge of a cliff; they perished by diseases brought on by terrible privation, and aggravated by the savage orgies with which it was varied.

Yet there was not only much that was attractive in their wild, free, reckless lives, but there was also very much good about the men themselves. They were—and such of them as are left still are—frank, bold, and self-reliant to a degree. They fear neither man, brute, nor element. They are generous and hospitable; they stand loyally by their friends, and pursue their enemies with bitter and vindictive hatred. For the rest, they

differ among themselves in their good and bad points even more mark-
edly than do men in civilized life, for out on the border virtue and wickedness alike take on very pronounced colors. A man who in civilization
would be merely a backbiter becomes a murderer on the frontier; and, on
the other hand, he who in the city would do nothing more than bid you a
cheery good-morning, shares his last bit of sun-jerked venison with you
when threatened by starvation in the wilderness. One hunter may be a
dark-browed, evil-eyed ruffian, ready to kill cattle or run off horses without hesitation, who if game fails will at once, in Western phrase, "take to
the road,"—that is, become a highwayman. The next is perhaps a quiet,
kindly, simple-hearted man, law-abiding, modestly unconscious of the
worth of his own fearless courage and iron endurance, always faithful to
his friends, and full of chivalric and tender loyalty to women.

The hunter is the arch-type of freedom. His well-being rests in no
man's hands save his own. He chops down and hews out the logs for his
hut, or perhaps makes merely a rude dug-out in the side of a hill, with a
skin roof, and skin flaps for the door. He buys a little flour and salt, and
in times of plenty also sugar and tea; but not much, for it must all be
carried hundreds of miles on the backs of his shaggy pack-ponies. In one
corner of the hut, a bunk covered with deer-skins forms his bed; a kettle
and a frying-pan may be all his cooking-utensils. When he can get no
fresh meat he falls back on his stock of jerked venison, dried in long strips
over the fire or in the sun.

Most of the trappers are Americans, but they also include some
Frenchmen and half-breeds. Both of the last, if on the plains, occasionally make use of queer wooden carts, very rude in shape, with stout
wheels that make a most doleful squeaking. In old times they all had
Indian wives; but nowadays those who live among and intermarry with
the Indians are looked down upon by the other frontiersmen, who con-
temptuously term them "squaw men." All of them depend upon their
rifles only for food and for self-defense, and make their living by trapping,
peltries being very valuable and yet not bulky. They are good game
shots, especially the pure Americans; although, of course, they are very
boastful, and generally stretch the truth tremendously in telling about
their own marksmanship. Still they often do very remarkable shooting,
both for speed and accuracy. One of their feats, that I never could learn
to copy, is to make excellent shooting after nightfall. Of course all this
applies only to the regular hunters; not to the numerous pretenders
who hang around the outskirts of the towns to try to persuade unwary
strangers to take them for guides.

14

On one of my trips to the mountains I happened to come across several old-style hunters at the same time. Two were on their way out of the woods, after having been all winter and spring without seeing a white

A FRENCH-CANADIAN TRAPPER.

face. They had been lucky, and their battered pack-saddles carried bales of valuable furs—fisher, sable, otter, mink, beaver. The two men, though fast friends and allies for many years, contrasted oddly. One was a short, square-built, good-humored Kanuck, always laughing and talking, who interlarded his conversation with a singularly original mixture of the most villainous French and English profanity. His partner was an American, gray-eyed, tall and straight as a young pine, with a saturnine, rather haughty face, and proud bearing. He spoke very little, and then in low tones, never using an oath; but he showed now and then a most unexpected sense of dry humor. Both were images of bronzed and rugged strength. Neither had the slightest touch of the bully in his nature; they treated others with the respect that they also exacted for themselves. They bore an excellent reputation as being not only highly skilled in woodcraft and the use of the rifle, but also men of tried courage and strict integrity, whose word could be always implicitly trusted.

I had with me at the time a hunter who, though their equal as marksman or woodsman, was their exact opposite morally. He was a pleasant companion and useful assistant, being very hard-working, and possessing a temper that never was ruffled by anything. He was also a good-looking fellow, with honest brown eyes; but he no more knew the difference between right and wrong than Adam did before the fall. Had he been at all conscious of his wickedness, or had he possessed the least sense of shame, he would have been unbearable as a companion; but he was so perfectly pleasant and easy, so good-humoredly tolerant of virtue in others, and he so wholly lacked even a glimmering suspicion that murder, theft, and adultery were matters of anything more than individual taste, that I actually grew to be rather fond of him. He never related any of his past deeds of wickedness as matters either for boastfulness or for regret; they were simply repeated incidentally in the course of conversation. Thus once, in speaking of the profits of his different enterprises, he casually mentioned making a good deal of money as a Government scout in the South-west by buying cartridges from some negro troops at a cent apiece and selling them to the hostile Apaches for a dollar each. His conduct was not due to sympathy with the Indians, for it appeared that later on he had taken part in massacring some of these same Apaches when they were prisoners. He brushed aside as irrelevant one or two questions which I put to him: matters of sentiment were not to be mixed up with a purely mercantile speculation. Another time we were talking of the curious angles bullets sometimes fly off at when they ricochet. To illustrate the matter he related an experience which I shall try to give in his own words. "One time, when I was keeping a saloon down in New Mexico, there was a man owed me a grudge. Well, he took sick of the small-pox, and the doctor told him he'd sure die, and he said if that was so he reckoned he'd kill me first. So he come a-riding in with his gun [in the West a revolver is generally called a gun] and begun shooting; but I hit him first, and away he rode. I started to get on my horse to follow him; but there was a little Irishman there who said he'd never killed a man, and he begged hard for me to give him my gun and let him go after the other man and finish him. So I let him go; and when he caught up, blamed if the little cuss did n't get so nervous that he fired off into the ground, and the darned bullet struck a crowbar, and glanced up, and hit the other man square in the head and killed him! Now, that *was* a funny shot, was n't it?"

The fourth member of our party round the camp-fire that night was a powerfully built trapper, partly French by blood, who wore a gayly colored capote, or blanket-coat, a greasy fur cap, and moccasins. He had grizzled hair, and a certain uneasy, half-furtive look about the eyes. Once or twice he showed a curious reluctance about allowing a man to approach him suddenly from behind. Altogether his actions were so odd that I felt some curiosity to learn his history. It turned out that he had been through a rather uncanny experience the winter before. He and another man had gone into a remote basin, or inclosed valley, in the heart of the mountains, where game was very plentiful; indeed, it was so abundant that they decided to pass the winter there. Accordingly they put up a log-cabin, working hard, and merely killing enough meat for their immediate use. Just as it was finished winter set in with tremendous snow-storms. Going out to hunt, in the first lull, they found, to their consternation, that every head of game had left the valley. Not an animal was to be found therein; they had abandoned it for their winter haunts. The outlook for the two adventurers was appalling. They were afraid of trying to break out through the deep snow-drifts, and starvation stared them in the face if they staid. The man I met had his dog with him. They put themselves on very short commons, so as to use up their flour as slowly as possible, and hunted unweariedly, but saw nothing. Soon a violent quarrel broke out between them. The other man, a fierce, sullen fellow, insisted that the dog should be killed, but the owner was exceedingly attached to it, and refused. For a couple of weeks they spoke no word to each other, though cooped in the little narrow pen of logs. Then one night the owner of the dog was wakened by the animal crying out; the other man had tried to kill it with his knife, but failed. The provisions were now almost exhausted, and the two men were glaring at each other with the rage of maddened, ravening hunger. Neither dared to sleep, for fear that the other would kill him. Then the one who owned the dog at last spoke, and proposed that, to give each a chance for his life, they should separate. He would take half of the handful of flour that was left and start off to try to get home; the other should stay where he was; and if he tried to follow the first, he was warned that he would be shot without mercy. A like fate was to be the portion of the wanderer if driven to return to the hut. The arrangement was agreed to and the two men separated, neither daring to turn his back while they were within rifle-shot of each other. For two days the one who went off toiled on with weary weakness through the snow-drifts. Late on the second afternoon, as he looked back from a high ridge, he saw in the far distance a black

A FIGHT IN THE STREET.

speck against the snow, coming along on his trail. His companion was dogging his footsteps. Immediately he followed his own trail back a little and lay in ambush. At dusk his companion came stealthily up, rifle in hand, peering cautiously ahead, his drawn face showing the starved, eager ferocity of a wild beast, and the man he was hunting shot him down exactly as if he had been one. Leaving the body where it fell, the wanderer continued his journey, the dog staggering painfully behind him. The next evening he baked his last cake and divided it with the dog. In the morning, with his belt drawn still tighter round his skeleton body, he once more set out, with apparently only a few hours of dull misery between him and death. At noon he crossed the track of a huge timber-wolf; instantly the dog gave tongue, and, rallying its strength, ran along the trail. The man struggled after. At last his strength gave out and he sat down to die; but while sitting still, slowly stiffening with the cold, he heard the dog baying in the woods. Shaking off his mortal numbness, he crawled towards the sound, and found the wolf over the body of a deer that he had just killed, and keeping the dog from it. At the approach of the new assailant the wolf sullenly drew off, and man and dog tore the raw deer-flesh with hideous eagerness. It made them very sick for the next twenty-four hours; but, lying by the carcass for two or three days, they recovered strength. A week afterwards the trapper reached a miner's cabin in safety. There he told his tale, and the unknown man who alone might possibly have contradicted it lay dead in the depths of the wolf-haunted forest.

The cowboys, who have supplanted these old hunters and trappers as the typical men of the plains, themselves lead lives that are almost as full of hardship and adventure. The unbearable cold of winter sometimes makes the small outlying camps fairly uninhabitable if fuel runs short; and if the line riders are caught in a blizzard while making their way to the home ranch, they are lucky if they get off with nothing worse than frozen feet and faces.

They are, in the main, hard-working, faithful fellows, but of course are frequently obliged to get into scrapes through no fault of their own. Once, while out on a wagon trip, I got caught while camped by a spring on the prairie, through my horses all straying. A few miles off was the camp of two cowboys, who were riding the line for a great Southern cow-outfit. I did not even know their names, but happening to pass by them I told of my loss, and the day after they turned up with the missing horses, which they had been hunting for twenty-four hours. All I could do in return was to give them some reading matter—something for which the men in these lonely camps are always grateful. Afterwards I spent a day or two with my new friends, and we became quite intimate. They were Texans. Both were quiet, clean-cut, pleasant-spoken young fellows, who did not even swear, except under great provocation,—and there can be no greater provocation than is given by a "mean" horse or a refractory steer. Yet, to my surprise, I found that they were, in a certain sense, fugitives from justice. They were complaining of the extreme severity of the winter weather, and mentioned their longing to go back to the South. The reason they could not was that the summer before they had taken part in a small civil war in one of the wilder counties of New Mexico. It had originated in a quarrel between two great ranches over their respective water rights and range rights,—a quarrel of a kind rife among pastoral peoples since the days when the herdsmen of Lot and Abraham strove together for the grazing lands round the mouth of the Jordan. There were collisions between bands of armed cowboys, the cattle were harried from the springs, outlying camps were burned down, and the sons of the rival owners fought each other to the death with bowie-knife and revolver when they met at the drinking-booths of the squalid towns. Soon the smoldering jealousy which is ever existent between the Americans and Mexicans of the frontier was aroused, and when the original cause of quarrel was adjusted, a fierce race struggle took its place. It was soon quelled by the arrival of a strong sheriff's posse and the threat of interference by the regular troops, but not until after a couple of affrays, each attended with bloodshed. In one of these the American cowboys of a certain range, after a brisk fight, drove out the Mexican *vaqueros* from among them. In the other, to avenge the murder of one of their number, the cowboys gathered from the country round about and fairly stormed the "Greaser" (that is, Mexican) village where the murder had been committed, killing four of the inhabitants. My two friends had borne a part in this last affair. They were careful to give a rather cloudy account of the details, but I gathered that one of them was "wanted" as a participant, and the other as a witness.

However, they were both good fellows, and probably their conduct was justifiable, at least according to the rather fitful lights of the border. Sitting up late with them, around the sputtering fire, they became quite confidential. At first our conversation touched only the usual monotonous round of subjects worn threadbare in every cow-camp. A bunch of steers had been seen traveling over the scoria buttes to the head of Elk Creek; they were mostly Texan *doughgies* (a name I have never seen written; it applies to young immigrant cattle), but there were some of the Hash-Knife four-year-olds among them. A stray horse with a blurred brand on the left hip had just joined the bunch of saddle-ponies. The red F. V. cow, one of whose legs had been badly bitten by a wolf, had got mired down in an alkali spring, and when hauled out had charged upon her rescuer so viciously that he barely escaped. The old mule, Sawback, was getting over the effects of the rattlesnake bite. The river was going down, but the fords were still bad, and the quicksand at the Custer Trail crossing had worked along so that wagons had to be taken over opposite the blasted cottonwood. One of the men had seen a Three-Seven-B rider who had just left the Green River round-up, and who brought news that they had found some cattle on the reservation, and were now holding about twelve hundred head on the big brushy bottom below Rainy Butte. Bronco Jim, our local flash rider, had tried to ride the big, bald-faced sorrel belonging to the Oregon horse-outfit, and had been bucked off and his face smashed in. This piece of information of course drew forth much condemnation of the unfortunate Jim's equestrian skill. It was at once agreed that he "was n't the sure-enough bronco-buster he thought himself," and he was compared very unfavorably to various heroes of the quirt and spurs who lived in Texas and Colorado; for the best rider, like the best hunter, is invariably either dead or else a resident of some other district.

These topics having been exhausted, we discussed the rumor that the vigilantes had given notice to quit to two men who had just built a shack at the head of the Little Dry, and whose horses included a suspiciously large number of different brands, most of them blurred. Then our conversation became more personal, and they asked if I would take some letters to post for them. Of course I said yes, and two letters—evidently the product of severe manual labor—were produced. Each was directed to a girl; and my companions, now very friendly, told me that they both had sweethearts, and for the next hour I listened to a full account of their charms and virtues.

But it is not often that plainsmen talk so freely. They are rather reserved, especially to strangers; and are certain to look with dislike on any man who, when they first meet him, talks a great deal. It is always a good plan, if visiting a strange camp or ranch, to be as silent as possible.

Another time, at a ranch not far from my own, I found among the cowboys gathered for the round-up two Bible-reading Methodists. They were as strait-laced as any of their kind, but did not obtrude their opinions on any one else, and were first-class workers, so that they had no trouble with the other men. Associated with them were two or three blear-eyed, slit-mouthed ruffians, who were as loose of tongue as of life.

Generally some form of stable government is provided for the counties as soon as their population has become at all fixed, the frontiersmen showing their national aptitude for organization. Then lawlessness is put down pretty effectively. For example, as soon as we organized the government of Medora — an excessively unattractive little hamlet, the county seat of our huge, scantily settled county — we elected some good officers, built a log jail, prohibited all shooting in the streets, and enforced the prohibition, etc., etc.

Up to that time there had been a good deal of lawlessness of one kind or another, only checked by an occasional piece of individual retribution or by a sporadic outburst of vigilance committee work. In such a society the desperadoes of every grade flourish. Many are merely ordinary rogues and swindlers, who rob and cheat on occasion, but are dangerous only when led by some villain of real intellectual power. The gambler, with hawk eyes and lissome fingers, is scarcely classed as a criminal; indeed, he may be a very public-spirited citizen. But as his trade is so often plied in saloons, and as even if, as sometimes happens, he does not cheat, many of his opponents are certain to attempt to do so, he is of necessity obliged to be skillful and ready with his weapon, and gambling rows are very common. Cowboys lose much of their money to gamblers; it is with them hard come and light go, for they exchange the wages of six months' grinding toil and lonely peril for three days' whooping carousal, spending their money on poisonous whisky or losing it over greasy cards in the vile dance-houses. As already explained, they are in the main good men; and the disturbance they cause in a town is done from sheer rough light-heartedness. They shoot off boot-heels or tall hats occasionally, or make some obnoxious butt "dance" by shooting round his feet; but they rarely meddle in this way with men who have not themselves

MAKING A TENDERFOOT DANCE.

played the fool. A fight in the streets is almost always a duel between two men who bear each other malice; it is only in a general mêlée in a saloon that outsiders often get hurt, and then it is their own fault, for they have no business to be there. One evening at Medora a cowboy spurred his horse up the steps of a rickety "hotel" piazza into the bar-room, where he began firing at the clock, the decanters, etc., the bartender meanwhile taking one shot at him, which missed. When he had emptied his revolver he threw down a roll of bank-notes on the counter, to pay for the damage he had done, and galloped his horse out through the door, disappearing in the darkness with loud yells to a rattling accompaniment of pistol shots interchanged between himself and some passer-by who apparently began firing out of pure desire to enter into the spirit of the occasion,—for it was the night of the Fourth of July, and all the country round about had come into town for a spree.

PAINTING THE TOWN RED.

All this is mere horse-play; it is the cowboy's method of "painting the town red," as an interlude in his harsh, monotonous life. Of course there are plenty of hard characters among cowboys, but no more than among lumbermen and the like; only the cowboys are so ready with their weapons that a bully in one of their camps is apt to be a murderer instead of merely a bruiser. Often, moreover, on a long trail, or in a far-off camp, where the men are for many months alone, feuds spring up that are in the end sure to be slaked in blood. As a rule, however, cowboys who become desperadoes soon perforce drop their original business, and are no longer employed on ranches, unless in counties or territories where there is very little heed paid to the law, and where, in consequence, a cattle-owner needs a certain number of hired bravos. Until within two or three years this was the case in parts of Arizona and New Mexico, where land claims were "jumped" and cattle stolen all the while, one effect being to insure high wages to every individual who combined murderous proclivities with skill in the use of the six-shooter.

Even in much more quiet regions different outfits vary greatly as regards the character of their employés: I know one or two where the men are good ropers and riders, but a gambling, brawling, hard-drinking set, always shooting each other or strangers. Generally, in such a case, the boss is himself as objectionable as his men; he is one of those who have risen by unblushing rascality, and is always sharply watched by his neighbors, because he is sure to try to shift calves on to his own cows, to brand any blurred animal with his own mark, and perhaps to attempt the alteration of perfectly plain brands. The last operation, however, has become very risky since the organization of the cattle country, and the appointment of trained brand-readers as inspectors. These inspectors examine the hide of every animal slain, sold, or driven off, and it is wonderful to see how quickly one of them will detect any signs of a brand having been tampered with. Now there is, in consequence, very little of this kind of dishonesty; whereas formerly herds were occasionally stolen almost bodily.

Claim-jumpers are, as a rule, merely blackmailers. Sometimes they will by threats drive an ignorant foreigner from his claim, but never an old frontiersman. They delight to squat down beside ranchmen who are themselves trying to keep land to which they are not entitled, and who therefore know that their only hope is to bribe or to bully the intruder.

Cattle-thieves, for the reason given above, are not common, although there are plenty of vicious, shiftless men who will kill a cow or a steer for the meat in winter, if they get a chance.

Horse-thieves, however, are always numerous and formidable on the frontier; though in our own country they have been summarily thinned out of late years. It is the fashion to laugh at the severity with which horse-stealing is punished on the border, but the reasons are evident. Horses are the most valuable property of the frontiersman, whether cowboy, hunter, or settler, and are often absolutely essential to his well-being, and even to his life. They are always marketable, and they are very easily stolen, for they carry themselves off, instead of having to be carried. Horse-stealing is thus a most tempting business, especially to the more reckless ruffians, and it is always followed by armed men; and they can only be kept in check by ruthless severity. Frequently they band together with the road agents (highwaymen) and other desperadoes into secret organizations, which control and terrorize a district until overthrown by force. After the civil war a great many guerrillas, notably from Arkansas and Missouri, went out to the plains, often drifting northward. They took naturally to horse-stealing and kindred pursuits. Since I have been in the northern cattle country I have known of half a dozen former members of Quantrell's gang being hung or shot.

The professional man-killers, or "bad men," may be horse-thieves or highwaymen, but more often are neither one nor the other. Some of them, like some of the Texan cowboys, become very expert in the use of the revolver, their invariable standby; but in the open a cool man with a rifle is always an overmatch for one of them, unless at very close quarters, on account of the superiority of his weapon. Some of the "bad men" are quiet, good fellows, who have been driven into their career by accident. One of them has perhaps at some time killed a man in self-defense; he acquires some reputation, and the neighboring bullies get to look on him as a rival whom it would be an honor to slay; so that from that time on he must be ever on the watch, must learn to draw quick and shoot straight, — the former being even more important than the latter,—and probably has to take life after life in order to save his own.

Some of these men are brave only because of their confidence in their own skill and strength; once convince them that they are overmatched and they turn into abject cowards. Others have nerves of steel and will face any odds, or certain death itself, without flinching a hand's breadth. I was once staying in a town where a desperately plucky fight took place. A noted desperado, an Arkansas man, had become involved in a quarrel with two others of the same ilk, both Irishmen and partners. For several days all three lurked about the saloon-infested streets of the roaring little board-and-canvas "city," each trying to get "the drop,"— that is, the first shot,— the other inhabitants looking forward to the fight with pleased curiosity, no one dreaming of interfering. At last one of the partners got a chance at his opponent as the latter was walking into a gambling hell, and broke his back near the hips; yet the crippled, mortally wounded man twisted around as he fell and shot his slayer dead. Then, knowing that he had but a few moments to live, and expecting that his other foe would run up on hearing the shooting, he dragged himself by his arms out into the street; immediately afterwards, as he anticipated, the second partner appeared, and was killed on the spot. The victor did not live twenty minutes. As in most of these encounters, all of the men who were killed deserved their fate. In my own not very extensive experience I can recall but one man killed in these fights whose death was regretted, and he was slain by a European. Generally every one is heartily glad to hear of the death of either of the contestants, and the only regret is that the other survives.

One curious shooting scrape that took place in Medora was worthy of being chronicled by Bret Harte. It occurred in the summer of 1884, I believe, but it may have been the year following. I did not see the actual occurrence, but I saw both men immediately afterwards; and I

A ROW IN A CATTLE TOWN.

heard the shooting, which took place in a saloon on the bank, while I was swimming my horse across the river, holding my rifle up so as not to wet it. I will not give their full names, as I am not certain what has become of them; though I was told that one had since been either put in jail or hung, I forget which. One of them was a saloon-keeper, familiarly called Welshy. The other man, Hay, had been bickering with him for some time. One day Hay, who had been defeated in a wrestling match by one of my own boys, and was out of temper, entered the other's saloon, and became very abusive. The quarrel grew more and more violent, and suddenly Welshy whipped out his revolver and blazed away at Hay. The latter staggered slightly, shook himself, stretched out his hand, and *gave back to his would-*

be slayer the ball, saying, "Here, man, here's the bullet." It had glanced along his breast-bone, gone into the body, and come out at the point of the shoulder, when, being spent, it dropped down the sleeve into his hand. Next day the local paper, which rejoiced in the title of "The Bad Lands Cowboy," chronicled the event in the usual vague way as an "unfortunate occurrence" between "two of our most esteemed fellow-citizens." The editor was a good fellow, a college graduate, and a first-class base-ball player, who always stood stoutly up against any corrupt dealing; but, like all other editors in small Western towns, he was intimate with both combatants in almost every fight.

The winter after this occurrence I was away, and on my return began asking my foreman—a particular crony of mine—about the fates of my various friends. Among others I inquired after a traveling preacher who had come to our neighborhood; a good man, but irascible. After a moment's pause a gleam of remembrance came into my informant's eye: "Oh, the parson! Well—he beat a man over the head with an ax, and they put him in jail!" It certainly seemed a rather summary method of repressing a refractory parishioner. Another acquaintance had shared a like doom. "He started to go out of the country, but they ketched him at Bismarck and put him in jail"—apparently on general principles, for I did not hear of his having committed any specific crime. My foreman sometimes developed his own theories of propriety. I remember his objecting strenuously to a proposal to lynch a certain French-Canadian who had lived in his own cabin, back from the river, ever since the whites came into the land, but who was suspected of being a horse-thief. His chief point against the proposal was, not that the man was innocent, but that "it did n't seem anyways right to hang a man who had been so long in the country."

Sometimes we had a comic row. There was one huge man from Missouri called "The Pike," who had been the keeper of a wood-yard for steamboats on the Upper Missouri. Like most of his class he was a hard case, and, though pleasant enough when sober, always insisted on fighting when drunk. One day, when on a spree, he announced his intention of thrashing the entire population of Medora seriatim, and began to make his promise good with great vigor and praiseworthy impartiality. He was victorious over the first two or three eminent citizens whom he encountered, and then tackled a gentleman known as "Cold Turkey Bill." Under ordinary circumstances Cold Turkey, though an able-bodied man, was no match for The Pike; but the latter was still rather drunk, and moreover was wearied by his previous combats. So Cold Turkey got him down, lay on him, choked him by the throat with one hand, and began pounding his face with a triangular rock held in the other. To the onlookers the fate of the battle seemed decided; but Cold Turkey better appreciated the endurance of his adversary, and it soon appeared that he sympathized with the traditional hunter who, having caught a wildcat, earnestly besought a comrade to help him let it go. While still pounding vigorously he raised an agonized wail: "Help me off, fellows, for the Lord's sake; he's tiring me out!" There was no resisting so plaintive an appeal, and the bystanders at once abandoned their attitude of neutrality for one of armed intervention.

I have always been treated with the utmost courtesy by all cowboys, whether on the round-up or in camp; and the few real desperadoes I have seen were also perfectly polite. Indeed, I never was shot at maliciously but once. This was on an occasion when I had to pass the night in a little frontier hotel where the bar-room occupied the whole lower floor, and was in consequence the place where every one, drunk or sober, had to sit. My assailant was neither a cowboy nor a *bona fide* "bad man," but a broad-hatted ruffian of cheap and commonplace type, who had for the moment terrorized the other men in the bar-room, these being mostly sheep-herders and small grangers. The fact that I wore glasses, together with my evident desire to avoid a fight, apparently gave him the impression—a mistaken one—that I would not resent an injury.

The first deadly affray that took place in our town, after the cattle-men came in and regular settlement began, was between a Scotchman and a Minnesota man, the latter being one of the small stockmen. Both had "shooting" records, and each was a man with a varied past. The Scotchman, a noted bully, was the more daring of the two, but he was much too hot-headed and overbearing to be a match for his gray-eyed, hard-featured foe. After a furious quarrel and threats of violence, the Scotchman mounted his horse, and, rifle in hand, rode to the door of the mud ranch, perched on the brink of the river-bluff, where the American lived, and was instantly shot down by the latter from behind a corner of the building.

Later on I once opened a cowboy ball with the wife of the victor in this contest, the husband himself dancing opposite. It was the lanciers, and he knew all the steps far better than I did. He could have danced a minuet very well with a little practice. The scene reminded one of the ball where Bret Harte's heroine "danced down the middle with the man who shot Sandy Magee."

But though there were plenty of men present each of whom had shot his luckless Sandy Magee, yet there was no Lily of Poverty Flat. There is an old and true border saying that "the frontier is hard on women and cattle." There are some striking exceptions; but, as a rule, the grinding

THE MAGIC OF THE DROP.

toil and hardship of a life passed in the wilderness, or on its outskirts, drive the beauty and bloom from a woman's face long before her youth has left her. By the time she is a mother she is sinewy and angular, with thin, compressed lips and furrowed, sallow brow. But she has a hundred qualities that atone for the grace she lacks. She is a good mother and a hard-working housewife, always putting things to rights, washing and cooking for her stalwart spouse and offspring. She is faithful to her husband, and, like the true American that she is, exacts faithfulness in return. Peril cannot daunt her, nor hardship and poverty appall her. Whether on the mountains in a log hut chinked with moss, in a sod or adobe hovel on the desolate prairie, or in a mere temporary camp, where the white-topped wagons have been drawn up in a protection-giving circle near some spring, she is equally at home. Clad in a dingy gown and a hideous sun-bonnet she goes bravely about her work, resolute, silent, uncomplaining. The children grow up pretty much as fate dictates. Even when very small they seem well able to protect themselves. The wife of one of my teamsters, who lived in a small outlying camp, used to keep the youngest and most troublesome members of her family out of mischief by the simple expedient of picketing them out, each child being tied by the leg, with a long leather string, to a stake driven into the ground, so that it could neither get at another child nor at anything breakable.

The best buckskin maker I ever met was, if not a typical frontiers-woman, at least a woman who could not have reached her full development save on the border. She made first-class hunting-shirts, leggins, and gauntlets. When I knew her she was living alone in her cabin on mid-prairie, having dismissed her husband six months previously in an exceed-ingly summary manner. She not only possessed redoubtable qualities of head and hand, but also a nice sense of justice, even towards Indians, that is not always found on the frontier. Once, going there for a buckskin shirt, I met at her cabin three Sioux, and from their leader, named One Bull, purchased a tobacco-pouch, beautifully worked with porcupine quills. She had given them some dinner, for which they had paid with a deer-hide. Falling into conversation, she mentioned that just before I came up a white man, apparently from Deadwood, had passed by, and had tried to steal the Indians' horses. The latter had been too quick for him, had run him down, and brought him back to the cabin. "I told 'em to go right on and hang him, and *I* would n't never cheep about it," said my informant; "but they let him go, after taking his gun. There ain't no sense in steal-ing from Indians any more than from white folks, and I'm not going to have it round my ranch, neither. There! I'll give 'em back the deer-hide they give me for the dinner and things, anyway." I told her I sincerely wished we could make her sheriff and Indian agent. She made the Indians —and whites, too, for that matter—behave themselves and walk the straightest kind of line, not tolerating the least symptom of rebellion; but she had a strong natural sense of justice.

The cowboy balls, spoken of above, are always great events in the small towns where they take place, being usually given when the round-up passes near; everybody round about comes in for them. They are almost always conducted with great decorum; no unseemly conduct would be tolerated. There is usually some master of the ceremonies, chosen with due regard to brawn as well as brain. He calls off the fig-ures of the square dances, so that even the inexperienced may get through them, and incidentally preserves order. Sometimes we are allowed to wear our revolvers, and sometimes not. The nature of the band, of course, depends upon the size of the place. I remember one ball that came near being a failure because our half-breed fiddler "went and got himself shot," as the indignant master of the ceremonies phrased it.

16

But all these things are merely incidents in the cowboy's life. It is utterly unfair to judge the whole class by what a few individuals do in the course of two or three days spent in town, instead of by the long months of weary, honest toil common to all alike. To appreciate properly his fine, manly qualities, the wild rough-rider of the plains should be seen in his own home. There he passes his days, there he does his life-work, there, when he meets death, he faces it as he has faced many other evils, with quiet, uncomplaining fortitude. Brave, hospitable, hardy, and adventurous, he is the grim pioneer of our race; he prepares the way for the civilization from before whose face he must himself disappear. Hard and dangerous though his existence is, it has yet a wild attraction that strongly draws to it his bold, free spirit. He lives in the lonely lands where mighty rivers twist in long reaches between the barren bluffs; where the prairies stretch out into billowy plains of waving grass, girt only by the blue horizon,—plains across whose endless breadth he can steer his course for days and weeks and see neither man to speak to nor hill to break the level; where the glory and the burning splendor of the sunsets kindle the blue vault of heaven and the level brown earth till they merge together in an ocean of flaming fire.

WHICH IS THE BAD MAN?

RED AND WHITE ON THE BORDER

THE SIGN LANGUAGE.

VII

RED AND WHITE ON THE BORDER

UP to 1880 the country through which the Little
Missouri flows remained as wild and almost as
unknown as it was when the old explorers and
fur traders crossed it in the early part of the
century. It was the last great Indian hunting-
ground, across which Grosventres and Mandans,
Sioux and Cheyennes, and even Crows and Rees wandered in
chase of game, and where they fought one another and plundered the small parties of white trappers and hunters that
occasionally ventured into it. Once or twice generals like
Sully and Custer had penetrated it in the course of the long,
tedious, and bloody campaigns that finally broke the strength
of the northern Horse Indians; indeed, the trail made by
Custer's baggage train is to this day one of the well-known
landmarks, for the deep ruts worn by the wheels of the
heavy wagons are in many places still as distinctly to be seen
as ever.

In 1883, a regular long-range skirmish took place just
south of us between some Cheyennes and some cowboys, with bloodshed
on both sides, while about the same time a band of Sioux plundered a
party of buffalo hunters of everything they owned, and some Crows who
attempted the same feat with another party were driven off with the loss of
two of their number. Since then there have been in our neighborhood no
stand-up fights or regular raids; but the Indians have at different times
proved more or less troublesome, burning the grass, and occasionally killing stock or carrying off horses that have wandered some distance away.
They have also themselves suffered somewhat at the hands of white
horse-thieves.

Bands of them, accompanied by their squaws and children, often come into the ranch country, either to trade or to hunt, and are then, of course, perfectly meek and peaceable. If they stay any time they build themselves quite comfortable tepees (wigwams, as they would be styled in the East), and an Indian camp is a rather interesting, though very dirty, place to visit. On our ranch we get along particularly well with them, as it is a rule that they shall be treated as fairly as if they were whites: we neither wrong them ourselves nor allow others to wrong them. We have always, for example, been as keen in putting down horse-stealing from Indians as from whites—which indicates rather an advanced stage of frontier morality, as theft from the "redskins" or the "Government" is usually held to be a very trivial matter compared with the heinous crime of theft from "citizens."

There is always danger in meeting a band of young bucks in lonely, uninhabited country—those that have barely reached manhood being the most truculent, insolent, and reckless. A man meeting such a party runs great risk of losing his horse, his rifle, and all else he has. This has happened quite frequently during the past few years to hunters or cowboys who have wandered into the debatable territory where our country borders on the Indian lands; and in at least one such instance, that took place three years ago, the unfortunate individual lost his life as well as his belongings. But a frontiersman of any experience can generally "stand off" a small number of such assailants, unless he loses his nerve or is taken by surprise.

My only adventure with Indians was of a very mild kind. It was in the course of a solitary trip to the north and east of our range, to what was then practically unknown country, although now containing many herds of cattle. One morning I had been traveling along the edge of the prairie, and about noon I rode Manitou up a slight rise and came out on a plateau that was perhaps half a mile broad. When near the middle, four or five Indians suddenly came up over the edge, directly in front of me. The second they saw me they whipped their guns out of their slings, started their horses into a run, and came on at full tilt, whooping and brandishing their weapons. I instantly reined up and dismounted. The level plain where we were was of all places the one on which such an onslaught could best be met. In any broken country, or where there is much cover, a white man is at a great disadvantage if pitted against such adepts in the art of hiding as Indians; while, on the other hand, the latter will rarely rush in on a foe who, even if overpowered in the end, will probably inflict severe loss on his assailants. The fury of an Indian charge, and the whoops by which it is accompanied, often scare horses so as to stampede them; but in Manitou I had perfect trust, and the old fellow stood as steady as a rock, merely cocking his ears and looking round at the noise. I waited until the Indians were a hundred yards off, and then threw up my rifle and drew a bead on the foremost. The effect

STANDING OFF INDIANS.

was like magic. The whole party scattered out as wild pigeons or teal ducks sometimes do when shot at, and doubled back on their tracks, the men bending over alongside their horses. When some distance off they halted and gathered together to consult, and after a minute one came forward alone, ostentatiously dropping his rifle and waving a blanket over his head. When he came to within fifty yards I stopped him, and he pulled out a piece of paper—all Indians, when absent from their reservations, are supposed to carry passes—and called out, "How! Me good Indian!" I answered, "How," and assured him most sincerely I was very glad he *was* a good Indian, but I would not let him come closer; and when his companions began to draw near, I covered him with the rifle and made him move off, which he did with a sudden lapse into the most canonical

Anglo-Saxon profanity. I then started to lead my horse out to the prairie; and after hovering round a short time they rode off, while I followed suit, but in the opposite direction. It had all passed too quickly for me to have time to get frightened; but during the rest of my ride I was exceedingly uneasy, and pushed tough, speedy old Manitou along at a rapid rate, keeping well out on the level. However, I never saw the Indians again. They may not have intended any mischief beyond giving me a fright; but I did not dare to let them come to close quarters, for they would have probably taken my horse and rifle, and not impossibly my scalp as well. Towards nightfall I fell in with two old trappers who lived near Killdeer Mountains, and they informed me that my assailants were some young Sioux bucks, at whose hands they themselves had just suffered the loss of two horses.

A few cool, resolute whites, well armed, can generally beat back a much larger number of Indians if attacked in the open. One of the first cattle outfits that came to the Powder River country, at the very end of the last war with the Sioux and Cheyennes, had an experience of this sort. There were six or eight whites, including the foreman, who was part owner, and they had about a thousand head of cattle. These they intended to hold just out of the dangerous district until the end of the war, which was evidently close at hand. They would thus get first choice of the new grazing grounds. But they ventured a little too far, and one day while on the trail were suddenly charged by fifty or sixty Indians. The cattle were scattered in every direction, and many of them slain in wantonness, though most were subsequently recovered. All the loose horses were driven off. But the men themselves instantly ran together and formed a ring, fighting from behind the pack and saddle ponies. One of their number was killed, as well as two or three of the animals composing their living breastwork; but being good riflemen, they drove off their foes. The latter did not charge them directly, but circled round, each rider concealed on the outside of his horse; and though their firing was very rapid, it was, naturally, very wild. The whites killed a good many ponies, and got one scalp, belonging to a young Sioux brave who dashed up too close, and whose body in consequence could not be carried off by his comrades, as happened to the two or three others who were seen to fall. Both the men who related the incident to me had been especially struck by the skill and daring shown by the Indians in thus carrying off their dead and wounded the instant they fell.

The relations between the white borderers and their red-skinned foes and neighbors are rarely pleasant. There are incessant quarrels, and each side has to complain of bitter wrongs. Many of the frontiersmen are brutal, reckless, and overbearing; most of the Indians are treacherous, revengeful, and fiendishly cruel. Crime and bloodshed are the only possible results when such men are brought in contact. Writers usually pay heed only to one side of the story; they recite the crimes committed by one party, whether whites or Indians, and omit all reference to the equally numerous sins of the other. In our dealings with the Indians we have erred quite as often through sentimentality as through willful wrong-doing. Out of my own short experience I could recite a dozen instances of white outrages which, if told alone, would seem to justify all the outcry raised on behalf of the Indian; and I could also tell of as many Indian atrocities which make one almost feel that not a single one of the race should be left alive.

The chief trouble arises from the feeling alluded to in this last sentence — the tendency on each side to hold the race, and not the individual, responsible for the deeds of the latter. The skirmish between the cowboys and the Cheyennes, spoken of above, offers a case in point. It was afterwards found out that two horse-thieves had stolen some ponies from the Cheyennes. The latter at once sallied out and attempted to take some from a cow camp, and a fight resulted. In exactly the same way I once knew a party of buffalo hunters, who had been robbed of their horses by the Sioux, to retaliate by stealing an equal number from some perfectly peaceful Grosventres. A white or an Indian who would not himself commit any outrage will yet make no effort to prevent his fellows from organizing expeditions against men of the rival race. This is natural enough where law is weak, and where, in consequence, every man has as much as he can do to protect himself without meddling in the quarrels of his neighbors. Thus a white community will often refrain from taking active steps against men who steal horses only from the Indians, although I have known a number of instances where the ranchmen have themselves stopped such outrages. The Indians behave in the same way. There is a peaceful tribe not very far from us which harbors two or three red horse-thieves, who steal from the whites at every chance. Recently, in our country, an expedition was raised to go against these horse-thieves, and it was only with the utmost difficulty that it was stopped: had it actually gone, accompanied as it would have been by scoundrels bent on plunder, as well as by wronged men who thought all redskins pretty much alike, the inevitable result would have been a bloody fight with all the Indians, both good and bad.

Not only do Indians differ individually, but they differ as tribes. An

17

AN EPISODE IN THE OPENING UP OF A CATTLE COUNTRY.

upper-class Cherokee is nowadays as good as a white. The Nez Percés differ from the Apaches as much as a Scotch laird does from a Calabrian bandit. A Cheyenne warrior is one of the most redoubtable foes in the whole world; a "digger" Snake one of the most despicable. The Pueblo is as thrifty, industrious, and peaceful as any European peasant, and no Arab of the Soudan is a lazier, wilder robber than is the Arapahoe.

The frontiersmen themselves differ almost as widely from one another. But in the event of an Indian outbreak all suffer alike, and so all are obliged to stand together: when the reprisals for a deed of guilt are sure to fall on the innocent, the latter have no resource save to ally themselves with the guilty. Moreover, even the best Indians are very apt to have a good deal of the wild beast in them; when they scent blood they wish their share of it, no matter from whose veins it flows. I once had a German in my employ, who, when a young child, had lost all his relations by a fate so terrible that it had weighed down his whole after-life. His family was living out on the extreme border at the time of the great Sioux outbreak towards the end of the civil war. There were many Indians around, seemingly on good terms with them; and to two of these Indians they had been able to be of much service, so that they became great friends. When the outbreak occurred, the members of this family were among the first captured. The two friendly Indians then endeavored to save their lives, doing all they could to dissuade their comrades from committing violence. Finally, after an angry discussion, the chief, who was present, suddenly ended it by braining the mother. The two former friends then, finding their efforts useless, forthwith turned round and joined with the others, first in violating the wretched daughters, and then in putting them to death with tortures that cannot even be hinted at. The boy alone was allowed to live. If he had been a native-born frontiersman, instead of a peaceful, quiet German, he probably would have turned into an inveterate Indian-slayer, resolute to kill any of the hated race wherever and whenever met—a type far from unknown on the border, of which I have myself seen at least one example.

With this incident it is only fair to contrast another that I heard related while spending the night in a small cow ranch on the Beaver, whither I had ridden on one of our many tedious hunts after lost horses. Being tired, I got into my bunk early, and while lying there listened to the conversation of two cowboys—both strangers to me—who had also ridden up to the ranch to spend the night. They were speaking of Indians, and mentioned, certainly without any marked disapprobation, a jury that had just acquitted a noted horse-thief of the charge of stealing stock from some Piegans, though he himself had openly admitted its truth. One, an unprepossessing, beetle-browed man, suddenly remarked that he had once met an Indian who was a pretty good fellow, and he proceeded to tell the story. A small party of Indians had passed the winter near the ranch at which he was employed. The chief had two particularly fine horses, which so excited his cupidity that one night he drove them off and "cached"—that is, hid—them in a safe place. The chief looked for them high and low, but without success. Soon afterwards one of the cowboy's own horses strayed. When spring came the Indians went away; but three days afterwards the chief returned, bringing with him the strayed horse, which he had happened to run across. "I could n't stand that," said the narrator, "so I just told him I reckoned I knew where his own lost horses were, and I saddled up my bronch' and piloted him to them."

Here and there on the border there is a certain amount of mixture with the Indian blood; much more than is commonly supposed. One of the most hard-working and prosperous men in our neighborhood is a Chippewa half-breed; he is married to a white wife, and ranks in every respect as a white. Two of our richest cattle-men are married to Indian women; their children are being educated in convents. In several of the most thriving North-western cities men could be pointed out, standing high in the community, who have a strong dash of Indian blood in their veins. Often, however, especially in the lower classes, they seem to feel some shame about admitting the cross, so that in a couple of generations it is forgotten.

Indians are excellent fighters, though they do not shoot well—being in this respect much inferior not only to the old hunters, but also, nowadays, to the regular soldiers, who during the past three or four years have improved wonderfully in marksmanship. They have a very effective discipline of their own, and thus a body of them may readily be an over-match for an equal number of frontiersmen if the latter have no leader whom they respect. If the cowboys have rifles—for the revolver is useless in long-range individual fighting—they feel no fear of the Indians, so long as there are but half a dozen or so on a side; but, though infinitely quicker in their movements than regular cavalry, yet, owing to their heavy saddles, they are not able to make quite so wonderful marches as the Indians do, and their unruly spirit often renders them ineffective when gathered in any number without a competent captain. Under a man like Forrest they would become the most formidable fighting horsemen in the world.

In the summer of 1886, at the time of the war-scare over the "Cutting incident," we began the organization of a troop of cavalry in our district, notifying the Secretary of War that we were at the service of the Government, and being promised every assistance by our excellent chief executive of the Territory, Governor Pierce.   Of course the cowboys were all eager for war, they did not much care with whom; they were very patriotic,* they were fond of adventure, and, to tell the truth, they were by no means averse to the prospect of plunder.   News from the outside world came to us very irregularly, and often in distorted form, so that we began to think we might get involved in a conflict not only with Mexico, but with England also.   One evening at my ranch the men began talking over the English soldiers, so I got down " Napier " and read them several extracts from his descriptions of the fighting in the Spanish peninsula, also recounting as well as I could the great deeds of the British cavalry from Waterloo to Balaklava, and finishing up by describing from memory the fine appearance, the magnificent equipment, and the superb horses of the Household cavalry and of a regiment of hussars I had once seen.

All of this produced much the same effect on my listeners that the sight of Marmion's cavalcade produced in the minds of the Scotch moss-troopers on the eve of Flodden; and at the end, one of them, who had been looking into the fire and rubbing his hands together, said with regretful emphasis, " Oh, how I *would* like to kill one of them ! "

* The day that the Anarchists were hung in Chicago, my men joined with the rest of the neighborhood in burning them in effigy.

ONE OF THE BOYS.

THE INDIAN PONY.

SHERIFF'S WORK ON A RANCH

AN OLD-TIME MOUNTAIN MAN WITH HIS PONIES.

VIII

SHERIFF'S WORK ON A RANCH

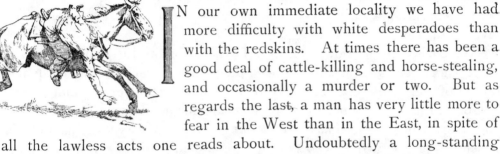

IN our own immediate locality we have had more difficulty with white desperadoes than with the redskins. At times there has been a good deal of cattle-killing and horse-stealing, and occasionally a murder or two. But as regards the last, a man has very little more to fear in the West than in the East, in spite of all the lawless acts one reads about. Undoubtedly a long-standing quarrel sometimes ends in a shooting-match; and of course savage affrays occasionally take place in the bar-rooms; in which, be it remarked, that, inasmuch as the men are generally drunk, and, furthermore, as the revolver is at best a rather inaccurate weapon, outsiders are nearly as apt to get hurt as are the participants. But if a man minds his own business and does not go into bar-rooms, gambling saloons, and the like, he need have no fear of being molested; while a revolver is a mere foolish incumbrance for any but a trained expert, and need never be carried. Against horse-thieves, cattle-thieves, claim-jumpers, and the like, however, every ranchman has to be on his guard; and armed collisions with these gentry are sometimes inevitable. The fact of such scoundrels being able to ply their trade with impunity for any length of time can only be understood if the absolute wildness of our land is taken into account. The country is yet unsurveyed and unmapped; the course of the river itself, as put down on the various Government and railroad maps, is very much a mere piece of guesswork, its bed being in many parts—as by my ranch—ten or fifteen miles, or more, away from where these maps make it. White hunters came into the land by 1880; but the actual settlement only began in 1882, when the first cattle-men drove in their herds, all of Northern stock, the Texans not passing north of the country around the head-waters of the river until the following year, while until 1885 the territory through which it ran for the final hundred and fifty miles before entering the Big Missouri remained as little known as ever.

Some of us had always been anxious to run down the river in a boat during the time of the spring floods, as we thought we might get good duck and goose shooting, and also kill some beaver, while the trip would, in addition, have all the charm of an exploring expedition. Twice, so far as we knew, the feat had been performed, both times by hunters, and in one instance with very good luck in shooting and trapping. A third attempt, by two men on a raft, made the spring preceding that on which we made ours, had been less successful; for, when a score or so of miles below our ranch, a bear killed one of the two adventurers, and the survivor returned.

We could only go down during a freshet; for the Little Missouri, like most plains' rivers, is usually either a dwindling streamlet, a mere slender thread of sluggish water, or else a boiling, muddy torrent, running over a bed of shifting quicksand, that neither man nor beast can cross. It rises and falls with extraordinary suddenness and intensity, an instance of which has just occurred as this very page is being written. Last evening, when the moon rose, from the ranch veranda we could see the river-bed almost dry, the stream having shrunk under the drought till it was little but a string of shallow pools, with between them a trickle of water that was not ankle deep, and hardly wet the fetlocks of the saddle-band when driven across it; yet at daybreak this morning, without any rain having fallen near us, but doubtless in consequence of some heavy cloudburst near its head, the swift, swollen current was foaming brim high between the banks, and even the fords were swimming-deep for the horses.

Accordingly we had planned to run down the river sometime towards the end of April, taking advantage of a rise; but an accident made us start three or four weeks sooner than we had intended.

In 1886 the ice went out of the upper river very early, during the first part of February; but it at times almost froze over again, the bottom ice did not break up, and a huge gorge, scores of miles in length, formed in and above the bend known as the Ox-bow, a long distance up-stream from my ranch. About the middle of March this great Ox-bow jam came down past us. It moved slowly, its front forming a high, crumbling wall, and creaming over like an immense breaker on the seashore: we could hear the dull roaring and crunching as it plowed down the river-bed long before it came in sight round the bend above us. The ice kept piling and tossing up in the middle, and not only heaped itself above the level of the banks, but also in many places spread out on each side beyond them, grinding against the cottonwood trees in front of the ranch veranda, and at one moment bidding fair to overwhelm the house itself. It did not, however, but moved slowly down past us with that look of vast, resistless, relentless force that any great body of moving ice, as a glacier, or an iceberg, always conveys to the beholder. The heaviest pressure from the water that was backed up behind being, of course, always in the middle, this part kept breaking away, and finally was pushed on clear through, leaving the river so changed that it could hardly be known. On each bank, and for a couple of hundred feet out from it into the stream, was a solid mass of ice, edging the river along most of its length, at least as far as its course lay through lands that we knew; and in the narrow channel between the sheer ice-walls the water ran like a mill-race.

At night the snowy, glittering masses, tossed up and heaped into fantastic forms, shone like crystal in the moonlight; but they soon lost their beauty, becoming fouled and blackened, and at the same time melted and settled down until it was possible to clamber out across the slippery hummocks.

We had brought out a clinker-built boat especially to ferry ourselves over the river when it was high, and were keeping our ponies on the opposite side, where there was a good range shut in by some very broken country that we knew they would not be apt to cross. This boat had already proved very useful and now came in handier than ever, as without it we could take no care of our horses. We kept it on the bank, tied to a tree, and every day would carry it or slide it across the hither ice bank, usually with not a little tumbling and scrambling on our part, lower it gently into the swift current, pole it across to the ice on the farther bank, and then drag it over that, repeating the operation when we came back. One day we crossed and walked off about ten miles to a tract of wild and rugged country, cleft in every direction by ravines and cedar cañons, in the deepest of which we had left four deer hanging a fortnight before, as game thus hung up in cold weather keeps indefinitely. The walking was very bad, especially over the clay buttes; for the sun at midday had enough strength to thaw out the soil to the depth of a few inches only, and accordingly the steep hillsides were covered by a crust of slippery mud, with the frozen ground underneath. It was hard to keep one's footing, and to avoid falling while balancing along the knife-like ridge crests, or while clinging to the stunted sage brush as we went down into the valleys. The deer had been hung in a thicket of dwarfed cedars; but when we reached the place we found nothing save scattered pieces of their carcasses, and the soft mud was tramped all over with round, deeply marked footprints, some of them but a few hours old, showing that the plunderers of our cache were a pair of cougars—"mountain lions," as they are called by the Westerners. They had evidently been at work for some time, and had eaten almost every scrap of flesh; one of the deer had been carried for some distance to the other side of a deep, narrow, chasm-like gully across which the cougar must have leaped with the carcass in its mouth. We followed the fresh trail of the cougars for some time, as it was well marked, especially in the snow still remaining in the bottoms of the deeper ravines; finally it led into a tangle of rocky hills riven by dark cedar-clad gorges, in which we lost it, and we retraced our steps, intending to return on the morrow with a good track hound.

But we never carried out our intentions, for next morning one of my men who was out before breakfast came back to the house with the start-ling news that our boat was gone—stolen, for he brought with him the end of the rope with which it had been tied, evidently cut off with a sharp knife; and also a red woolen mitten with a leather palm, which he had picked up on the ice. We had no doubt as to who had stolen it; for whoever had done so had certainly gone down the river in it, and the only other thing in the shape of a boat on the Little Missouri was a small flat-bottomed scow in the possession of three hard characters who lived in a shack, or hut, some twenty miles above us, and whom we had shrewdly suspected for some time of wishing to get out of the country, as certain of the cattle-men had begun openly to threaten to lynch them. They belonged to a class that always holds sway during the raw youth of a frontier com-munity, and the putting down of which is the first step towards decent gov-ernment. Dakota, west of the Missouri, has been settled very recently, and every town within it has seen strange antics performed during the past six or seven years. Medora, in particular, has had more than its full share of shooting and stabbing affrays, horse-stealing, and cattle-killing. But the time for such things was passing away; and during the preceding fall the vigilantes—locally known as "stranglers," in happy allusion to their summary method of doing justice—had made a clean sweep of the cattle country along the Yellowstone and that part of the Big Missouri around and below its mouth. Be it remarked, in passing, that while the outcome of their efforts had been in the main wholesome, yet, as is always the case in an extended raid of vigilantes, several of the sixty odd victims had been perfectly innocent men who had been hung or shot in company with the real scoundrels, either through carelessness and misapprehension or on account of some personal spite.

The three men we suspected had long been accused—justly or unjustly —of being implicated both in cattle-killing and in that worst of frontier crimes, horse-stealing: it was only by an accident that they had escaped the clutches of the vigilantes the preceding fall. Their leader was a well-built fellow named Finnigan, who had long red hair reaching to his shoulders, and always wore a broad hat and a fringed buckskin shirt. He was rather a hard case, and had been chief actor in a number of shooting scrapes. The other two were a half-breed, a stout, muscular man, and an old German, whose viciousness was of the weak and shiftless type.

We knew that these three men were becoming uneasy and were anxious to leave the locality; and we also knew that traveling on horseback, in the direction in which they would wish to go, was almost impossible, as the swollen, ice-fringed rivers could not be crossed at all, and the stretches of broken ground would form nearly as impassable barriers. So we had little doubt that it was they who had taken our boat; and as they knew there was then no boat left on the river, and as the country along its banks was entirely impracticable for horses, we felt sure they would be confident that there could be no pursuit.

Accordingly we at once set to work in our turn to build a flat-bottomed scow, wherein to follow them. Our loss was very annoying, and might prove a serious one if we were long prevented from crossing over to look after the saddle-band; but the determining motive in our minds was neither chagrin nor anxiety to recover our property. In any wild country where the power of the law is little felt or heeded, and where every one has to rely upon himself for protection, men soon get to feel that it is in the highest degree unwise to submit to any wrong without making an immediate and resolute effort to avenge it upon the wrong-doers, at no matter what cost of risk or trouble. To submit tamely and meekly to theft, or to any other injury, is to invite almost certain repetition of the offense, in a place where self-reliant hardihood and the ability to hold one's own under all circumstances rank as the first of virtues.

Two of my cowboys, Seawall and Dow, were originally from Maine, and were mighty men of their hands, skilled in woodcraft and the use of the ax, paddle, and rifle. They set to work with a will, and, as by good luck there were plenty of boards, in two or three days they had turned out a first-class flat-bottom, which was roomy, drew very little water, and was dry as a bone; and though, of course, not a handy craft, was easily enough managed in going down-stream. Into this we packed flour, coffee,

and bacon enough to last us a fortnight or so, plenty of warm bedding, and
the mess kit; and early one cold March morning slid it into the icy
current, took our seats, and shoved off down the river.

There could have been no better men for a trip of this kind than my
two companions, Seawall and Dow. They were tough, hardy, resolute
fellows, quick as cats, strong as bears, and able to travel like bull moose.
We felt very little uneasiness as to the result of a fight with the men we
were after, provided we had anything like a fair show; moreover, we
intended, if possible, to get them at such a disadvantage that there would
not be any fight at all. The only risk of any consequence that we ran was
that of being ambushed; for the extraordinary formation of the Bad Lands,
with the ground cut up into gullies, serried walls, and battlemented hill-
tops, makes it the country of all others for hiding-places and ambuscades.

For several days before we started the weather had been bitterly cold,
as a furious blizzard was blowing; but on the day we left there was a lull,
and we hoped a thaw had set in. We all were most warmly and thickly
dressed, with woolen socks and underclothes, heavy jackets and trousers,
and great fur coats, so that we felt we could bid defiance to the weather.
Each carried his rifle, and we had in addition a double-barreled duck gun,
for water-fowl and beaver. To manage the boat, we had paddles, heavy
oars, and long iron-shod poles, Seawall steering while Dow sat in the
bow. Altogether we felt as if we were off on a holiday trip, and set to
work to have as good a time as possible.

The river twisted in every direction, winding to and fro across the
alluvial valley bottom, only to be brought up by the rows of great barren
buttes that bounded it on each edge. It had worn away the sides of these
till they towered up as cliffs of clay, marl, or sandstone. Across their
white faces the seams of coal drew sharp black bands, and they were elsewhere blotched and varied with brown, yellow, purple, and red. This
fantastic coloring, together with the jagged irregularity of their crests,
channeled by the weather into spires, buttresses, and battlements, as well
as their barreness and the distinctness with which they loomed up through
the high, dry air, gave them a look that was a singular mixture of the
terrible and the grotesque. The bottoms were covered thickly with leafless cottonwood trees, or else with withered brown grass and stunted,
sprawling sage bushes. At times the cliffs rose close to us on either hand,
and again the valley would widen into a sinuous oval a mile or two long,
bounded on every side, as far as our eyes could see, by a bluff line without a break, until, as we floated down close to its other end, there would
suddenly appear in one corner a cleft through which the stream rushed
out. As it grew dusk the shadowy outlines of the buttes lost nothing of

their weirdness; the twilight only made their uncouth shapelessness more grim and forbidding. They looked like the crouching figures of great goblin beasts.

> Those two hills on the right
> Crouched like two bulls locked horn in horn in fight —
> While to the left a tall scalped mountain. . . .
> The dying sunset kindled through a cleft:
> The hills, like giants at a hunting, lay
> Chin upon hand, to see the game at bay —

might well have been written after seeing the strange, desolate lands lying in western Dakota.

All through the early part of the day we drifted swiftly down between the heaped-up piles of ice, the cakes and slabs now dirty and unattractive looking. Towards evening, however, there came long reaches where the banks on either side were bare, though even here there would every now and then be necks where the jam had been crowded into too narrow a spot and had risen over the side as it had done up-stream, grinding the bark from the big cottonwoods and snapping the smaller ones short off. In such places the ice-walls were sometimes eight or ten feet high, continually undermined by the restless current; and every now and then overhanging pieces would break off and slide into the stream with a loud sullen splash, like the plunge of some great water beast. Nor did we dare to go in too close to the high cliffs, as bowlders and earth masses, freed by the thaw from the grip of the frost, kept rolling and leaping down their faces and forced us to keep a sharp lookout lest our boat should be swamped.

THE CAPTURE OF THE GERMAN.

At nightfall we landed, and made our camp on a point of wood-covered land jutting out into the stream. We had seen very little trace of life until late in the day, for the ducks had not yet arrived; but in the afternoon a sharp-tailed prairie fowl flew across stream ahead of the boat, lighting on a low branch by the water's edge. Shooting him, we landed and picked off two others that were perched high up in leafless cottonwoods, plucking the buds. These three birds served us as supper; and shortly afterward, as the cold grew more and more biting, we rolled in under our furs and blankets and were soon asleep.

In the morning it was evident that instead of thawing it had grown decidedly colder. The anchor ice was running thick in the river, and we spent the first hour or two after sunrise in hunting over the frozen swamp bottom for white-tail deer, of which there were many tracks; but we saw nothing. Then we broke camp and again started down-stream—a simple operation, as we had no tent, and all we had to do was to cord up our bedding and gather the mess kit. It was colder than before, and for some time we went along in chilly silence, nor was it until midday that the sun warmed our blood in the least. The crooked bed of the current twisted hither and thither, but whichever way it went the icy north wind, blowing stronger all the time, drew steadily up it. One of us remarking that we bade fair to have it in our faces all day, the steersman announced that we could n't, unless it was the crookedest wind in Dakota; and half an hour afterward we overheard him muttering to himself that it *was* the crookedest wind in Dakota. We passed a group of tepees on one bottom, marking the deserted winter camp of some Grosventre Indians, which some of my men had visited a few months previously on a trading expedition. It was almost the last point on the river with which we were acquainted. At midday we landed on a sand-bar for lunch—a simple enough meal, the tea being boiled over a fire of driftwood, that also fried the bacon, while the bread only needed to be baked every other day. Then we again shoved off. As the afternoon waned the cold grew still more bitter, and the wind increased, blowing in fitful gusts against us, until it chilled us to the marrow when we sat still. But we rarely did sit still; for even the rapid current was unable to urge the light-draught scow down in the teeth of the strong blasts, and we only got her along by dint of hard work with pole and paddle. Long before the sun went down the ice had begun to freeze on the handles of the poles, and we were not sorry to haul on shore for the night. For supper we again had prairie fowl, having shot four from a great patch of bulberry bushes late in the afternoon. A man doing hard open-air work in cold weather is always hungry for meat.

During the night the thermometer went down to zero, and in the morning the anchor ice was running so thickly that we did not care to start at once, for it is most difficult to handle a boat in the deep frozen slush. Accordingly we took a couple of hours for a deer hunt, as there were evidently many white-tail on the bottom. We selected one long, isolated patch of tangled trees and brushwood, two of us beating through it while the other watched one end; but almost before we had begun four deer broke out at one side, loped easily off, evidently not much scared, and took refuge in a deep glen or gorge, densely wooded with cedars, that made a blind pocket in the steep side of one of the great plateaus bounding the bottom.   After a short consultation, one of our number crept round to the head of the gorge, making a wide détour, and the other two advanced up it on each side, thus completely surrounding the doomed deer.   They

"HANDS UP!"—THE CAPTURE OF FINNIGAN.

attempted to break out past the man at the head of the glen, who shot down a couple, a buck and a yearling doe.   The other two made their escape by running off over ground so rough that it looked fitter to be crossed by their upland-loving cousins, the black-tail.

This success gladdened our souls, insuring us plenty of fresh meat. We carried pretty much all of both deer back to camp, and, after a hearty breakfast, loaded our scow and started merrily off once more.   The cold still continued intense, and as the day wore away we became numbed by it, until at last an incident occurred that set our blood running freely again.

We were, of course, always on the alert, keeping a sharp lookout ahead and around us, and making as little noise as possible.   Finally our watchfulness was rewarded, for in the middle of the afternoon of this, the

19

third day we had been gone, as we came around a bend, we saw in front
of us the lost boat, together with a scow, moored against the bank, while
from among the bushes some little way back the smoke of a camp-fire
curled up through the frosty air. We had come on the camp of the thieves.
As I glanced at the faces of my two followers I was struck by the grim,
eager look in their eyes. Our overcoats were off in a second, and after
exchanging a few muttered words, the boat was hastily and silently shoved
towards the bank. As soon as it touched the shore ice I leaped out and
ran up behind a clump of bushes, so as to cover the landing of the others,
who had to make the boat fast. For a moment we felt a thrill of keen
excitement, and our veins tingled as we crept cautiously towards the fire,
for it seemed likely that there would be a brush; but, as it turned out, this
was almost the only moment of much interest, for the capture itself was as
tame as possible.

The men we were after knew they had taken with them the only craft
there was on the river, and so felt perfectly secure; accordingly, we took
them absolutely by surprise. The only one in camp was the German,
whose weapons were on the ground, and who, of course, gave up at once,
his two companions being off hunting. We made him safe, delegating one
of our number to look after him particularly and see that he made no noise,
and then sat down and waited for the others. The camp was under the lee
of a cut bank, behind which we crouched, and, after waiting an hour or
over, the men we were after came in. We heard them a long way off and
made ready, watching them for some minutes as they walked towards us,
their rifles on their shoulders and the sunlight glinting on the steel
barrels. When they were within twenty yards or so we straightened up
from behind the bank, covering them with our cocked rifles, while I
shouted to them to hold up their hands — an order that in such a case, in
the West, a man is not apt to disregard if he thinks the giver is in earnest.
The half-breed obeyed at once, his knees trembling as if they had been
made of whalebone. Finnigan hesitated for a second, his eyes fairly
wolfish; then, as I walked up within a few paces, covering the center of
his chest so as to avoid overshooting, and repeating the command, he saw
that he had no show, and, with an oath, let his rifle drop and held his
hands up beside his head.

It was nearly dusk, so we camped where we were. The first thing to
be done was to collect enough wood to enable us to keep a blazing fire all
night long. While Seawall and Dow, thoroughly at home in the use of
the ax, chopped down dead cottonwood trees and dragged the logs up
into a huge pile, I kept guard over the three prisoners, who were huddled

"TAKE OFF YOUR BOOTS!"

into a sullen group some twenty yards off, just the right distance for the buckshot in the double-barrel. Having captured our men, we were in a quandary how to keep them. The cold was so intense that to tie them tightly hand and foot meant, in all likelihood, freezing both hands and feet off during the night; and it was no use tying them at all unless we tied them tightly enough to stop in part the circulation. So nothing was left for us to do but to keep perpetual guard over them. Of course we had carefully searched them, and taken away not only their firearms and knives, but everything else that could possibly be used as a weapon. By this time they were pretty well cowed, as they found out very quickly that they would be well treated so long as they remained quiet, but would receive some rough handling if they attempted any disturbance.

Our next step was to cord their weapons up in some bedding, which we sat on while we took supper. Immediately afterward we made the men take off their boots—an additional safeguard, as it was a cactus country, in which a man could travel barefoot only at the risk of almost certainly laming himself for life—and go to bed, all three lying on one buffalo robe and being covered by another, in the full light of the blazing fire. We determined to watch in succession a half-night apiece, thus each getting a full

rest every third night.   I took first watch, my two companions, revolver
under head, rolling up in their blankets on the side of the fire opposite
that on which the three captives lay; while I, in fur cap, gantlets, and
overcoat, took my station a little way back in the circle of firelight, in a
position in which I could watch my men with the absolute certainty of

DOWN-STREAM.

being able to stop any movement, no matter how sudden.   For this night-
watching we always used the double-barrel with buckshot, as a rifle is
uncertain in the dark; while with a shot-gun at such a distance, and with
men lying down, a person who is watchful may be sure that they cannot
get up, no matter how quick they are, without being riddled.   The only
danger lies in the extreme monotony of sitting still in the dark guarding
men who make no motion, and the consequent tendency to go to sleep,
especially when one has had a hard day's work and is feeling really tired.
But neither on the first night nor on any subsequent one did we ever abate
a jot of our watchfulness.

   Next morning we started down-stream, having a well-laden flotilla,
for the men we had caught had a good deal of plunder in their boats,
including some saddles, as they evidently intended to get horses as soon
as they reached a part of the country where there were any, and where it
was possible to travel.   Finnigan, who was the ringleader, and the man I

was especially after, I kept by my side in our boat, the other two being put in their own scow, heavily laden and rather leaky, and with only one paddle. We kept them just in front of us, a few yards distant, the river being so broad that we knew, and they knew also, any attempt at escape to be perfectly hopeless.

For some miles we went swiftly down-stream, the cold being bitter and the slushy anchor ice choking the space between the boats; then the current grew sluggish, eddies forming along the sides. We paddled on until, coming into a long reach where the water was almost backed up, we saw there was a stoppage at the other end. Working up to this, it proved to be a small ice jam, through which we broke our way only to find ourselves, after a few hundred yards, stopped by another. We had hoped that the first was merely a jam of anchor ice, caused by the cold of the last few days; but the jam we had now come to was black and solid, and, running the boats ashore, one of us went off down the bank to find out what the matter was. On climbing a hill that commanded a view of the valley for several miles, the explanation became only too evident—as far as we could see, the river was choked with black ice. The great Ox-bow jam had stopped, and we had come down to its tail.

We had nothing to do but to pitch camp, after which we held a consultation. The Little Missouri has much too swift a current,—when it has any current at all,—with too bad a bottom, for it to be possible to take a boat up-stream; and to walk meant, of course, abandoning almost all we had. Moreover we knew that a thaw would very soon start the jam, and so made up our minds that we had best simply stay where we were, and work down-stream as fast as we could, trusting that the spell of bitter weather would pass before our food gave out.

The next eight days were as irksome and monotonous as any I ever spent: there is very little amusement in combining the functions of a sheriff with those of an arctic explorer. The weather kept as cold as ever. During the night the water in the pail would freeze solid. Ice formed all over the river, thickly along the banks; and the clear, frosty sun gave us so little warmth that the melting hardly began before noon. Each day the great jam would settle down-stream a few miles, only to wedge again, leaving behind it several smaller jams, through which we would work our way until we were as close to the tail of the large one as we dared to go. Once we came round a bend and got so near that we were in a good deal of danger of being sucked under. The current ran too fast to let us work back against it, and we could not pull the boat up over the steep banks of rotten ice, which were breaking off and falling in all the time. We could only land and snub the boats up with ropes, holding them there for two or three hours until the jam worked down once more — all the time, of course, having to keep guard over the captives, who had caused us so much trouble that we were bound to bring them in, no matter what else we lost.

We had to be additionally cautious on account of being in the Indian country, having worked down past Killdeer Mountains, where some of my cowboys had run across a band of Sioux—said to be Tetons—the year before. Very probably the Indians would not have harmed us anyhow, but as we were hampered by the prisoners, we preferred not meeting them; nor did we, though we saw plenty of fresh signs, and found, to our sorrow, that they had just made a grand hunt all down the river, and had killed or driven off almost every head of game in the country through which we were passing.

ON GUARD AT NIGHT.

As our stock of provisions grew scantier and scantier, we tried in vain to eke it out by the chase; for we saw no game. Two of us would go out hunting at a time, while the third kept guard over the prisoners. The latter would be made to sit down together on a blanket at one side of the fire, while the guard for the time being stood or sat some fifteen or twenty yards off. The prisoners being unarmed, and kept close together, there was no possibility of their escaping, and the guard kept at such a distance that they could not overpower him by springing on him, he having a Winchester or the double-barreled shot-gun always in his hands cocked and at the ready. So long as we kept wide-awake and watchful, there was not the least danger, as our three men knew us, and understood perfectly that the slightest attempt at a break would result in their being shot down; but, although there was thus no risk, it was harassing, tedious work, and the strain, day in and day out, without any rest or let up, became very tiresome.

The days were monotonous to a degree. The endless rows of hills bounding the valley, barren and naked, stretched along without a break. When we rounded a bend, it was only to see on each hand the same lines of broken buttes dwindling off into the distance ahead of us as they had dwindled off into the distance behind. If, in hunting, we climbed to their tops, as far as our eyes could scan there was nothing but the great rolling prairie, bleak and lifeless, reaching off to the horizon. We broke camp in the morning, on a point of land covered with brown, leafless, frozen cottonwoods; and in the afternoon we pitched camp on another point in the midst of a grove of the same stiff, dreary trees. The discolored river, whose eddies boiled into yellow foam, flowed always between the same banks of frozen mud or of muddy ice. And what was, from a practical standpoint, even worse, our diet began to be as same as the scenery. Being able to kill nothing, we exhausted all our stock of provisions, and got reduced to flour, without yeast or baking-powder; and unleavened bread, made with exceedingly muddy water, is not, as a steady thing, attractive.

Finding that they were well treated and were also watched with the closest vigilance, our prisoners behaved themselves excellently and gave no trouble, though afterward, when out of our hands and shut up in jail, the half-breed got into a stabbing affray. They conversed freely with my two men on a number of indifferent subjects, and after the first evening no allusion was made to the theft, or anything connected with it; so that an outsider overhearing the conversation would never have guessed what our relations to each other really were. Once, and once only, did Finnigan broach the subject. Somebody had been speaking of a man whom we all knew, called "Calamity," who had been recently taken by the sheriff on a charge of horse-stealing. Calamity had escaped once, but was caught at a disadvantage the next time; nevertheless, when summoned to hold his hands up, he refused, and attempted to draw his own revolver, with the result of having two bullets put through him. Finnigan commented on Calamity as a fool for "not knowing when a man had the drop on him"; and then, suddenly turning to me, said, his weather-beaten face flushing darkly: "If I 'd had any show at all, you 'd have sure had to fight, Mr. Roosevelt; but there was n't any use making a break when I 'd only have got shot myself, with no chance of harming any one else." I laughed and nodded, and the subject was dropped.

Indeed, if the time was tedious to us, it must have seemed never-ending to our prisoners, who had nothing to do but to lie still and read, or chew the bitter cud of their reflections, always conscious that some pair of eyes was watching them every moment, and that at least one loaded rifle was ever ready to be used against them. They had quite a stock of books, some of a rather unexpected kind. Dime novels and the inevitable "History of the James Brothers"—a book that, together with the "Police Gazette," is to be found in the hands of every professed or putative ruffian in the West—seemed perfectly in place; but it was somewhat surprising to find that a large number of more or less drearily silly "society" novels, ranging from Ouida's to those of The Duchess and Augusta J. Evans, were most greedily devoured. As for me, I had brought with me "Anna Karénina," and my surroundings were quite gray enough to harmonize well with Tolstoï.

Our commons grew shorter and shorter; and finally even the flour was nearly gone, and we were again forced to think seriously of abandoning the boats. The Indians had driven all the deer out of the country; occasionally we shot prairie fowl, but they were not plentiful. A flock of geese passed us one morning, and afterward an old gander settled down on the river near our camp; but he was over two hundred yards off, and a rifle-shot missed him. Where he settled down, by the way, the river was covered with thick glare ice that would just bear his weight; and it was curious to see him stretch his legs out in front and slide forty or fifty feet when he struck, balancing himself with his outspread wings.

But when the day was darkest the dawn appeared. At last, having worked down some thirty miles at the tail of the ice jam, we struck an outlying cow-camp of the C Diamond (C ◇) ranch, and knew that our troubles were almost over. There was but one cowboy in it, but we were certain of his cordial help, for in a stock country all make common cause against either horse-thieves or cattle-thieves. He had no wagon, but told us we could get one up at a ranch near Killdeer Mountains, some fifteen miles off, and lent me a pony to go up there and see about it — which I accordingly did, after a sharp preliminary tussle when I came to mount the wiry bronco (one of my men remarking in a loud aside to our cowboy host, "the boss ain't no bronco-buster"). When I reached the solitary ranch spoken of, I was able to hire a large prairie schooner and two tough little bronco mares, driven by the settler himself, a rugged old plainsman, who evidently could hardly understand why I took so much bother with the thieves instead of hanging them off-hand. Returning to the river the next day, we walked our men up to the Killdeer Mountains.

Seawall and Dow left me the following morning, went back to the boats, and had no further difficulty, for the weather set in very warm. the ice went through with a rush, and they reached Mandan in about ten days, killing four beaver and five geese on the way, but lacking time to stop to do any regular hunting.

"A SHARP PRELIMINARY TUSSLE."

Meanwhile I took the three thieves into Dickinson, the nearest town. The going was bad, and the little mares could only drag the wagon at a walk; so, though we drove during the daylight, it took us two days and a night to make the journey. It was a most desolate drive. The prairie had been burned the fall before, and was a mere bleak waste of blackened earth, and a cold, rainy mist lasted throughout the two days. The only variety was where the road crossed the shallow headwaters of Knife and Green rivers. Here the ice was high along the banks, and the wagon had to be taken to pieces to get it over. My three captives were unarmed, but as I was alone with them, except for the driver, of whom I knew nothing, I had to be doubly on my guard, and never let them come close to me. The little mares went so slowly, and the heavy road rendered any hope of escape by flogging up the horses so entirely out of the question, that I

20

soon found the safest plan was to put the prisoners in the wagon and myself walk behind with the inevitable Winchester. Accordingly I trudged steadily the whole time behind the wagon through the ankle-deep mud.

ON THE ROAD TO DICKINSON.

It was a gloomy walk. Hour after hour went by always the same, while I plodded along through the dreary landscape—hunger, cold, and fatigue struggling with a sense of dogged, weary resolution. At night, when we put up at the squalid hut of a frontier granger, the only habitation on our road, it was even worse. I did not dare to go to sleep, but making my three men get into the upper bunk, from which they could get out only with difficulty, I sat up with my back against the cabin-door and kept watch over them all night long. So, after thirty-six hours' sleeplessness, I was most heartily glad when we at last jolted into the long, straggling main street of Dickinson, and I was able to give my unwilling companions into the hands of the sheriff.

Under the laws of Dakota I received my fees as a deputy sheriff for making the three arrests, and also mileage for the three hundred odd miles gone over—a total of some fifty dollars.*

* One of the men wrote me from prison, giving me his reasons for taking the boat. Part of his letter is worth giving, not only because it contains his own story, but also for the sake of the deli-

cious sense of equality shown in the last few sentences. He had been explaining that he believed I had accused him of stealing some saddles: " In the first place I did not take your boat Mr. Roosevelt because I wanted to steal something, no indeed, when I took that vessel I was labouring under the impression, die dog or eat the hachette. . . . . When I was a couple of miles above your ranch the boat I had sprung a leak and I saw that I could not make the Big Missouri in it in the shape that it was in. I thought of asking assistance of you, but I supposed that you had lost some saddles and blamed me for taking them. Now there I was with a leaky boat and under the circumstances what was I two do, two ask you for help, the answer I expected two get was two look down the mouth of a Winchester. I saw your boat and made up my mind two get possession of it. I was bound two get out of that country cost what it might, when people talk lynch law and threaten a persons life, I think that it is about time two leave. I did not want to go back up river on the account that I feared a mob. . . . . I have read a good many of your sketches of ranch life in the papers since I have been here, and they interested me deeply.

" Yours sincerely,

" &c.

" P. S. Should you stop over at Bismarck this fall make a call to the Prison. I should be glad to meet you."

A TEXAN COWBOY.

AN AGENCY POLICEMAN.

THE RANCHMAN'S RIFLE ON CRAG
AND PRAIRIE

AN ELK.

IX

The Ranchman's Rifle on Crag and Prairie

HE ranchman owes to his rifle not only the keen pleasure and strong excitement of the chase, but also much of his bodily comfort; for, save for his prowess as a hunter and his skill as a marksman with this, his favorite weapon, he would almost always be sadly stinted for fresh meat. Now that the buffalo have gone, and the Sharps rifle by which they were destroyed is also gone, almost all ranchmen use some form of repeater. Personally I prefer the Winchester, using the new model, with a 45-caliber bullet of 300 grains, backed by 90 grains of powder, or else falling back on my faithful old stand-by, the 45–75. But the truth is that all good modern rifles are efficient weapons; it is the man behind the gun that makes the difference. An inch or two in trajectory or a second or two in rapidity of fire is as nothing compared to sureness of eye and steadiness of hand.

From April to August antelope are the game we chiefly follow, killing only the bucks; after that season, black-tail and white-tail deer. Now and then we get a chance at mountain sheep, and more rarely at larger game still. As a rule, I never shoot anything but bucks. But in the rutting season, when the bucks' flesh is poor, or when we need to lay in a good stock of meat for the winter, this rule of course must be broken.

The smoked venison stored away in the fall lasts us through the bitter weather, as well as through the even less attractive period covering the first weeks of spring. At that time we go out as little as possible. The roads are mere morasses, crusted after nightfall with a shell of thin ice, through which the shaggy horses break heavily. Walking is exceedingly tiresome, the boots becoming caked with masses of adhesive clay. The deer stay with us all the time; but they are now in poor condition, the does heavy with fawn and the bucks with ungrown antlers.

Antelope gather together in great bands in the fall, and either travel south, leaving the country altogether, or else go to some out-of-the-way place where they are not likely to be disturbed. Antelope are queer, freaky beasts, and it is hard to explain why, when most of these great bands go off south, one or two always stay in the Bad Lands. Such a band having chosen its wintering ground, which is usually in a valley or on a range of wide plateaus, will leave it only with great reluctance, and if it is discovered by hunters most of its members will surely be butchered before the survivors are willing to abandon the place and seek new quarters.

In April the prong-horned herds come back, but now all broken up into straggling parties. They have regular passes, through which they go every year: there is one such not far from my ranch, where they are certain to cross the Little Missouri in great numbers each spring on their return march. In the fall, when they are traveling in dense crowds, hunters posted in these passes sometimes butcher enormous numbers.

Soon after they come back in the spring they scatter out all over the plains, and for four months after their return—that is, until August—they are the game we chiefly follow. This is because at that time we only hunt enough to keep the ranch in fresh meat, and kill nothing but the bucks; and as antelope, though they shed their horns, are without them for but a very short time, and as, moreover, they are always seen at a distance, it is easy to tell the sexes apart.

Antelope shooting is the kind in which a man most needs skill in the use of the rifle at long ranges; for they are harder to get near than any other game—partly from their wariness, and still more from the nature of the ground they inhabit. Many more cartridges are spent, in proportion to the amount of game killed, in hunting antelope than is the case while after deer, elk, or sheep. Even good hunters reckon on using six or seven cartridges for every prong-horn that they kill; for antelope are continually offering standing shots at very long distances, which, nevertheless, it is a great temptation to try, on the chance of luck favoring the marksman. Moreover, alone among plains' game, they must generally be shot at over a hundred and fifty yards, and often at between two and three hundred. Over this distance a man will kill occasionally,—I have done so myself,—but at such long range it is mainly a matter of accident. The best field-shot alive lacks a good deal of always killing, if the distance is much over two hundred yards; and with every increase beyond that amount, the chances of failure augment in geometrical proportion. Exceptional individuals perform marvelous feats with the rifle, exactly as still more exceptional individuals perform marvelous feats with the revolver; but even these men, when they have to guess their distances, miss very often when firing at game three hundred yards, or thereabouts, distant.

As in all other kinds of big-game shooting, success in hunting antelope often depends upon sheer, downright luck. A man may make a week's trip over good ground and get nothing; and then again he may go to the same place and in two days kill a wagon-load of venison.

In the fall the prairie fires ravage the land, for at the close of summer the matted, sun-dried grass burns like tinder, and the fires are sometimes so numerous as to cover whole counties beneath a pall of smoke, while at night they look very grand, burning in curved lines of wavering flame, now advancing fastest at one point, now at another, as if great red snakes were writhing sideways across the prairie. The land across which they have run remains a blackened, charred waste until the young grass begins to sprout in the spring. The short, tender blades at once change the cinder-colored desert into a bright emerald plain, and are so much more toothsome than the dry, withered winter grass that both stock and game forsake the latter and travel out to the tracts of burned land. The feed on these places is too sparse to support, of itself, horses or cattle, who accordingly do not penetrate far beyond the edges; but antelope are like sheep, and prefer scanty, short herbage, and in consequence at this time fairly swarm in the burned districts. Indeed, they are sometimes so numerous that they can hardly be stalked, as it is impossible to approach any animal without being seen by some of its countless comrades, which at once run off and give the alarm.

While on these early spring trips we sometimes vary the sport, and our fare as well, by trying our rifles on the mallards in the reedy sloughs, or on the jack rabbits as they sit up on their haunches to look at us, eighty or a hundred yards off. Now and then we creep up to and kill the cock prairie fowl, when they have gathered into their dancing rings to posture with outstretched neck and outspread wings as they shuffle round each other, keeping up a curious clucking and booming that accord well with their grotesque attitudes.

Late in the season any one of us can usually get antelope in a day's hunt from the ranch by merely riding off alone, with a good hunting horse, to a great tract of broken, mound-dotted prairie some fifteen miles off, where the prong-horns are generally abundant.

On such a trip I leave the ranch house by dawn, the rifle across my saddle-bow, and some strips of smoked venison in the saddle-pockets. In

21

the cool air the horse lopes smartly through the wooded bottoms. The meadow-larks, with black crescents on their yellow breasts, sing all day long, but the thrushes only in the morning and evening; and their melody is heard at its best on such a ride as this. By the time I get out of the last ravines and canter along the divide, the dark bluff-tops in the east have begun to redden in the sunrise, while in the flushed west the hills stand out against a rosy sky. The sun has been up some little time before the hunting-grounds are fairly reached; for the antelope stands alone in being a diurnal game animal that from this peculiarity, as well as from the nature of its haunts, can be hunted as well at midday as at any other hour. Arrived at the hunting-grounds I generally, but not always, dismount and hunt on foot, leaving the horse tethered out to graze.

Lunch is taken at some spring, which may be only a trickle of water at the base of a butte, where a hole must be dug out with knife and hands before the horse can drink. Once or twice I have enjoyed unusual delicacies at such a lunch, in the shape of the eggs of curlew or prairie fowl baked in the hot ashes.

The day is spent in still-hunting, a much easier task among the ridges and low hills than out on the gently rolling prairies. Antelope see much better than deer, their great bulging eyes, placed at the roots of the horns, being as strong as twin telescopes. Extreme care must be taken not to let them catch a glimpse of the intruder, for it is then hopeless to attempt approaching them. On the other hand, there is never the least difficulty about seeing them; for they are conspicuous beasts, and, unlike deer, they never hide, being careless whether they are seen or not, so long as they can keep a good lookout. They trust only to their own alert watchfulness and quick senses for safety. The game is carried home behind the saddle; and the bottom on which the ranch house stands is not often reached until the moon, showing crimson through the haze, has risen above the bluffs that skirt the river.

Antelope are very tough, and will carry off a great deal of lead unless struck in exactly the right place; and even when mortally hit they sometimes receive the blow without flinching, and gallop off as if unharmed. They always should be followed up a little distance after being fired at, as if unhurt. Sometimes they show the rather curious trait of walking backwards a number of steps just before falling in death.

Although ordinarily harder to get at than deer, they are far more frequently killed in what may be called accidental ways. At times they seem to be heedless of danger, and they suffer from occasional panic fits of fear or curiosity, when it is no feat at all to slay them. Hunters can thus

BRINGING HOME THE GAME.

occasionally rake very large bags of antelope, but a true sportsman who only shoots for peculiarly fine trophies, or to supply the ranch table, will not commit such needless butcheries.   Often accidents have thrown it into my power to make a big killing; but the largest number I have ever shot was on one day when I bagged four, all bucks, and then we were sorely in need of fresh meat, and it was an object to get as much as possible. This day's shooting was peculiar because it took place during a heavy rain storm, which, taken in connection with my own remarkable costume, apparently made the animals act with less than their usual shyness.   I wore a great flapping yellow slicker, or oilskin overcoat, about as unlikely a garb as a hunter could possibly don; but it seemed to fascinate the game, for more than once a band huddled up and stood gazing at me, while I clambered awkwardly off the horse. The cold rain numbed my fingers and beat into my eyes, and I was hampered by the coat; so I wasted a good many cartridges to get my four head.

In some places they now seem to have learned wisdom, for the slaughter among them has been so prodigious that the survivors have radically changed their character. Their senses are as keen as ever, and their wits much keener. They no longer give way to bursts of panic curiosity; they cannot be attracted by any amount of flagging, or by the appearance of unknown objects, as formerly. Where they are still common, as with us, they refuse, under any stress of danger, to enter woodland or thickets, but keep to the flat or broken plains and the open prairies, which they have from time immemorial inhabited. But elsewhere their very nature seems to have altered. They have not only learned to climb and take to the hills, but, what is even more singular, have intruded on the domain of the elk and the deer, frequently making their abode in the thick timber, and there proving the most difficult of all animals to stalk.

In May and June the little antelope kids appear: funny little fellows, odd and ungainly, but at an astonishingly early age able to run nearly as fast as their parents. They will lie very close if they think that they are unobserved. Once several of us were driving in a herd of cattle while on the round-up. The cattle, traveling in loose order, were a few paces ahead, when, happening to cast down my eyes, I saw, right among their hoofs, a little antelope kid. It was lying flat down with outstretched neck, and did not move, although some of the cattle almost stepped on it. I reined up, got off my horse, and lifted it in my arms. At first it gave two or three convulsive struggles, bleating sharply, then became perfectly passive, standing quietly by me for a minute or two when I put it down, after which it suddenly darted off like a flash. These little antelope kids are very easily tamed, being then very familiar, amusing, and inquisitive — much more so than deer fawns, though they are not so pretty. Within a few days of their birth they stop seeking protection in hiding and adopt the habits of their parents, following them everywhere, or going off on their own account, being almost as swift, although, of course, not nearly so enduring.

Three of us witnessed a rather curious incident last spring, showing how little the bringing forth of a fawn affects the does of either deer or antelope. We were walking through a patch of low brushwood, when up got a black-tail doe and went off at full speed. At the second jump she gave birth to a fawn; but this did not alter her speed in the least, and she ran off quite as well and as fast as ever. We walked up to where she had been lying and found in her bed another fawn, evidently but a few seconds old. We left the two sprawling, unlicked little creatures where they were, knowing that the mother would soon be back to care for them.

Although sometimes we go out to the antelope ground and back in one day, yet it is always more convenient to take the buckboard with us and spend the night, camping by a water hole in one of the creeks. The last time we took such a trip I got lost, and nearly spent the night in the open. I had been riding with one of my cowboys, while another acted as teamster and drove the buckboard and pair. We killed two antelope and went into camp rather early. After taking dinner and picketing out the four horses we found it still lacked an hour or two of sunset, and accordingly my companions and I started out on foot, leaving our teamster in camp, and paying no particular heed to our surroundings. We saw a herd of prong-horn and wounded one, which we followed in vain until dusk, and then started to go back to camp. Very soon we found that we had quite a task before us, for in the dim starlight all the hollows looked exactly alike, and the buttes seemed either to have changed form entirely or else loomed up so vaguely through the darkness that we could not place them in the least. We walked on and on until we knew that we must be far past the creek, or coulée, where our camp lay, and then turned towards the divide. The night had grown steadily darker, and we could hear the far-off mutter and roll that told of an approaching thunder-storm. Hour after hour we trudged wearily on, as fast as we could go without stumbling, the gloom and the roughness of the unknown ground proving serious drawbacks to our progress. When on the top of a hillock, the blackness of the hollow beneath was so intense that we could not tell whether we were going to walk down a slope or over a cliff, and in consequence we met with one or two tumbles. At last we reached the top of a tall butte that we knew must be on the divide. The night was now as dark as pitch, and we were so entirely unable to tell where we were that we decided to give up the quest in despair and try to find some washout that would yield us at least partial shelter from the approaching rain storm. We had fired off our rifles several times without getting any response; but now, as we took one last look around, we suddenly saw a flash of light, evidently from a gun, flare up through the darkness so far off that no sound came to our ears. We trotted towards it as fast as we could through the inky gloom, and when no longer sure of our direction climbed a little hill, fired off our rifles, and after a minute or two again saw the guiding flash. The next time we had occasion to signal, the answering blaze was accompanied by a faint report; and

in a few minutes more, when it was close on midnight, we were warming our hands at the great camp-fire, and hungrily watching the venison
steaks as they sizzled in the frying-pan.

The morning after this adventure I shot an antelope before breakfast.
We had just risen, and while sitting round the smoldering coals, listen-

A PRONG-HORN BUCK VISITS CAMP.

ing to the simmering of the camp-kettle and the coffee-pot, we suddenly
caught sight of a large prong-horn buck that was walking towards us
over the hill-crest nearly half a mile away.   He stopped and stared fixedly at us for a few minutes, and then resumed his course at a leisurely
trot, occasionally stopping to crop a mouthful of grass, and paying no
further heed to us.   His course was one that would lead him within a
quarter of a mile of camp, and, grasping my rifle, I slipped off as soon as
he was out of sight and ran up over the bluff to intercept him.   Just as
I reached the last crest I saw the buck crossing in front of me at a walk,
and almost two hundred yards off.   I knelt, and, as he halted and turned
his head sharply towards me, pulled trigger.   It was a lucky shot, and he
fell over, with his back broken.   He had very unusually good horns; as
fine as those of any of his kind that I ever killed.

Antelope often suffer from such freaks of apathetic indifference to danger, which are doubly curious as existing in an animal normally as wary as that wildest of game, the mountain sheep.   They are fond of wandering too, and appear at times in very unlikely places.   Thus once, while we were building the cow corral, in an open bottom, five antelope came down.   After much snorting and stamping, they finally approached to within fifty yards of the men who were at work, and, as the latter had no weapons with them, retired unmolested.

In winter the great herds consist of the two sexes; and this is true also of the straggling parties that come back to us in spring, soon to split up into smaller ones.   During early summer the males may be found singly, or else three or four together, with possibly a barren doe or two; while two or three does, with their kids, and perhaps the last year's young, will form the nucleus of a little flock by themselves.   With the coming of the rutting season they divide into regular bands, for they are polygamous. Every large, powerful buck gathers his little group of does, driving out all his rivals, though perhaps a yearling buck or two will hang round the outskirts at a respectful distance, every now and then rousing the older one to a fit of jealous impatience.   More often the young bucks go in small parties by themselves, while those older ones that have been driven out by their successful rivals wander round singly.   The old bucks are truculent and courageous, and do fierce battle with each other until it is evident which is master, when the defeated combatant makes off at top speed.   One of these beaten bucks will occasionally get hold of a single doe, whom he promptly appropriates and guards with extreme watchfulness; and, not being overconfident in his own prowess, drives her off very rapidly if any other antelope show signs of coming near.   A successful buck may have from four or five to ten or fifteen does in his harem. In such a band there is always an old doe that acts as leader, precisely as with deer and elk.   This doe is ever on the alert, is most likely to take the alarm at the approach of danger, and always leads the flight.   The buck, however, is prompt to take command, if he sees fit, or deems that the doe's fears have overpowered her judgment; and frequently, when a band is in full flight, the buck may be seen deliberately to round it up and stop it, so that he may gaze on the cause of the alarm—a trait the exercise of which often costs him his life.   The bucks occasionally bully the does unmercifully, if they show symptoms of insubordination.   Individual antelope vary very widely in speed.   Once I fairly rode one down, but this is generally an almost impossible feat.   Among deer, the fat, heavy antlered bucks are usually slower than the does and the young males; but there seems to be little difference of this sort among prong-horns.

With the first touch of sharp fall weather we abandon the chase of the antelope for that of the deer. Then our favorite quarry is the noble black-tail, whose haunts are in the mountains and the high, craggy hills. We kill him by fair still-hunting, and to follow him successfully through the deep ravines and across the steep ridges of his upland home a man should be sound in wind and limbs, and a good shot with the rifle as well. Many a glorious fall morning I have passed in his pursuit; often, moreover, I have slain him in the fading evening as I walked homeward through the still dim twilight—for all wild game dearly love the gloaming.

Once on a frosty evening I thus killed one when it was so dark that my aim was little but guess-work. I was walking back to camp through a winding valley, hemmed in by steep cedar-crowned walls of clay and rock. All the landscape glimmered white with the new-fallen snow, and in the west the sky was still red with the wintry sunset. Suddenly a great buck came out of a grove of snow-laden cedars, and walked with swift strides up to the point of a crag that overlooked the valley. There he stood motionless while I crouched unseen in the shadow beneath. As I fired he reared upright and then plunged over the cliff. He fell a hundred feet before landing in the bushes, yet he did not gash or mar his finely molded head and shapely, massive antlers.

On one of the last days I hunted, in November, 1887, I killed two black-tail, a doe and a buck, with one bullet. They were feeding in a glen high up the side of some steep hills, and by a careful stalk over rough ground I got within fifty yards. Peering over the brink of the cliff-like slope up which I had clambered, I saw them standing in such a position that the neck of the doe covered the buck's shoulder. The chance was too tempting to be lost. My bullet broke the doe's neck, and of course she fell where she was; but the buck went off, my next two or three shots missing him. However, we followed his bloody trail, through the high pass he had crossed, down a steep slope, and roused him from the brush-wood in a valley bottom. He soon halted and lay down again, making off at a faltering gallop when approached, and the third time we came up to him he was too weak to rise. He had splendid antlers.

Sometimes we kill the deer by the aid of hounds. Of these we have two at the ranch. One is a rough-coated, pure-blood Scotch stag-hound, named Rob. The other, Brandy, is a track-hound, bell-mouthed, lop-eared, keen-nosed, and not particularly fast, but stanch as Death himself. He comes of the old Southern strain; and, indeed, all the best blooded packs of American deer-hounds or fox-hounds come from what was called the Southern Hound in early seventeenth century England. Thus he is kin to the hounds of Bellemeade, wherewith General Jackson follows the buck

and the gray fox over the beautiful fertile hills of middle Tennessee; and
some of the same blood runs in the veins of Mr. Wadsworth's Geneseo
hounds, behind which I have ridden as they chased the red fox through
the wooded glens and across the open fields of the farms, with their high
rail fences.

I often take Rob out when still-hunting black-tail, leading him along in
a leash. He is perfectly quiet, not even whimpering; and he is certain to

THE BUCK OVERTAKEN.

overhaul any wounded deer. A doe or a flying buck is borne to the ground
with a single wrench, and killed out of hand; but a buck at bay is a formidable opponent, and no dog can rush in full on the sharp prong points.
If the two dogs are together, Rob does most of the killing; Brandy's only
function is to distract the attention of an angry buck and then allow Rob
to pin him. Once a slightly wounded and very large black-tail buck, started
just at nightfall, ran down to the river and made a running bay of nearly
two hours, Rob steadily at him the whole time; it was too dark for us to
shoot, but finally, by a lucky throw, one of the men roped the quarry.

Not only will a big black-tail buck beat off a dog or a wolf coming at him in front, but he is an awkward foe for a man. One of them nearly killed a cowboy in my employ. The buck, mortally wounded, had fallen to the shot, and the man rushed up to stick him; then the buck revived for a moment, struck down the man, and endeavored to gore him, but could not, because of the despairing grip with which the man held on to his horns. Nevertheless the man, bruised and cut by the sharp hoofs, was fast becoming too weak to keep his hold, when in the struggle they came to the edge of a washout, and fell into it some twelve or fifteen feet. This separated them. The dying buck was too weak to renew the attack, and the man crawled off; but it was months before he got over the effects of the encounter.

Sometimes we kill the white-tail also by fair still-hunting, but more often we shoot them on the dense river bottoms by the help of the track-hound. We put the dogs into the woods with perhaps a single horseman to guide them and help them rout out the deer, while the rest of us, rifle in hand, ride from point to point outside, or else watch the passes through which the hunted animals are likely to run. It is not a sport of which I am very fond, but it is sometimes pleasant as a variety. The last time that we tried it I killed a buck in the bottom right below our ranch house, not half a mile off. The river was low, and my post was at its edge, with in front of me the broad sandy flat sparsely covered with willow-brush. Deer are not much afraid of an ordinary noisy hound; they will play round in front of him, head and flag in air; but with Rob it was different. The gray, wolfish beast, swift and silent, threw them into a panic of terror, and in headlong flight they would seek safety from him in the densest thicket.

On the evening in question one of my cowboys went into the brush with the hounds. I had hardly ridden to my place and dismounted when I heard old Brandy give tongue, the bluffs echoing back his long-drawn baying. Immediately afterwards a young buck appeared, coming along the sandy river-bed, trotting or cantering; and very handsome he looked, stepping with a light, high action, his glossy coat glistening, his head thrown back, his white flag flaunting. My bullet struck him too far back, and he went on, turning into the woods. Then the dogs appeared, old Brandy running the scent, while the eager gaze-hound made wide half-circles round him as he ran; while the cowboy, riding a vicious yellow mustang, galloped behind, cheering them on. As they struck the bloody trail they broke into clamorous yelling, and tore at full speed into the woods. A minute or two later the sound ceased, and I knew that they had run into the quarry.

Sometimes we use the hounds for other game besides deer. A neighboring ranchman had a half-breed fox-and-greyhound, who, single-handed, ran into and throttled a coyote.   I have been very anxious to try my dogs on a big wolf, intending to take along a collie and a half-breed mastiff we have to assist at the bay.   The mastiff is a good fighter, and can kill a wildcat, taking the necessary punishment well, as we found out when we once trapped one of these small lynxes.   Shep, the collie, is an adept at killing badgers, grabbing them from behind and whirling them round, whereas Brandy always gets his great lop-ears bitten.   But how they would do with a wolf I cannot say; for one of these long-toothed wanderers is usually able to outrun and outfight any reasonable number of common hounds, and will kill even a big dog very quickly.

A friend of mine, Mr. Heber Bishop, once coursed and killed a wolf with two Scotch deer-hounds.   After a brisk run the dogs overtook and held the quarry, but could not kill it, and were being very roughly handled when Mr. Bishop came to their assistance.   But a ranchman in the Indian Territory has a large pack of these same Scotch dogs trained especially to hunt the wolf; and four or five of the fleet, high-couraged animals can not only soon overhaul a wolf, but can collar and throttle even the largest.   Accidents to the pack are, of course, frequent.   They say that the worry is enough to make one's hair stand on end.

Before leaving the subject, it is worth noting that we have with us the Canada lynx as well as his smaller brother; and, more singular still, that a wolverine, usually found only in the northern forests, was killed two winters ago in a big woody bottom on the Little Missouri, about forty miles north of Medora.   The skin and skull were unmistakable; so there could be no doubt as to the beast's identity.

I have had good sport on the rolling plains, near Mandan, in following a scratch pack of four fleet, long-legged dogs.   One was a wire-haired Scotch deer-hound; his mate was a superb greyhound, the speediest of the set.   Both were possessed of the dauntless courage peculiar to high-bred hunting dogs. The other two were mongrels, but, nevertheless, game fighters and swift runners: one was a lurcher, and the other a cross between a greyhound and a fox-hound—the only one of the four that ever gave tongue. The two former had been used together often, and had slain five coyotes, two deer (white-tails), and an antelope.   Both the antelope and the deer they had fairly run down, having come up close on them, so that they had good send-offs; but there is a wide individual variation among game animals as regards speed, and those that they caught—at any rate the antelope—may not have been as fleet as most of their kind.   They were especially fond of chasing coyotes, and these they easily overtook.

When at bay the coyotes fought desperately but unavailingly, the two hounds killing their quarry very quickly, one seizing it by the throat and the other by the flanks, and then stretching it out in a trice. They occasionally received trifling injuries in these contests. The animal that gave them most trouble was a badger which they once found and only killed after prolonged efforts, its squat, muscular form and tough skin making it very difficult for them to get a good hold.

We did not have time to go far from Mandan, and so confined our coursing to jack rabbits, swifts, and foxes. Of the latter, the great red prairie fox, we saw but one, which got up so close to the dogs that it had no chance at all, and after a fine burst of a few hundred yards was overtaken and torn to pieces. The swifts are properly called swift foxes, being rather smaller than the southern gray fox. Ever since the days of the early explorers they have been reputed to possess marvelous speed, and their common name of "swift," by which they are universally known, perpetuates the delusion; for a delusion it emphatically is, since they are, if anything, rather slow than otherwise. Once, in a snow storm, I started one up under my horse's feet while riding across the prairie, overtook him in a few strides, and killed him by a lucky shot with the revolver. The speed of the coyote also has been laughably exaggerated. Judging by the records of the hounds, the antelope is the fastest plains' animal, the white-tail deer and the jack rabbit coming next; then follow, in order, the coyote, the fox, and the swift, which is the slowest of all. Individuals vary greatly, however; thus a fast jack rabbit might well outrun a slow deer, and of course both coyote and fox will outlast the swifter jack rabbits. Several dogs should run together, as otherwise a jack or a swift, although overtaken, may yet escape by its dexterity in dodging. The cactus beds often befriend the hunted animals, as the dogs rush heedlessly into them and are promptly disabled, while a rabbit or a fox will slip through without injury.

Two or three of us usually went out together. Our method of procedure was simple. We scattered out, dogs and men, and rode in an irregular line across the country, beating with care the most likely looking places, and following at top speed any game that got up. Sometimes a jack rabbit, starting well ahead, would run for two miles or over, nearly in a straight line, before being turned by the leading hound; and occasionally one would even get away altogether. At other times it would be overhauled at once and killed instantly, or only prolong its life a few seconds by its abrupt turns and twists. One swift gave us several minutes' chase, although never getting thirty rods from the place where it started. The little fellow went off as merrily as possible, his handsome brush streaming behind him, and, though overtaken at once, dodged so cleverly that dog after dog shot by him. I do not think that a single dog could have killed him.

Coursing is the sport of all sports for ranchmen, now that big animals are growing scarce; and certainly there can be no healthier or more exciting pastime than that of following game with horse and hound over the great Western plains.

OUR CAMP.

MOUNTAIN LIONS AT THE DEER CACHE.

THE WAPITI, OR ROUND-HORNED ELK

OUR ELK OUTFIT AT THE FORD.

X

THE WAPITI, OR ROUND-HORNED ELK

THIS stately and splendid deer, the lordliest of its kind throughout the world, is now fast vanishing. In our own neighborhood it is already almost a thing of the past. But a small band yet lingers round a great tract of prairie and Bad Lands some thirty-five miles from the ranch house.

One fall I killed a good bull out of the lot. I was hunting on horseback, and roused the elk out of a deep, narrow coulée, heavily timbered, where he was lying by himself. He went straight up the steep side directly opposite to where I stood, for I had leaped off my horse when I heard the crash of the underbrush. When on a level with me, he halted and turned half round to gaze at me across the ravine, and then I shot him.

The next season, when we were sorely in need of meat for smoking and drying, we went after these elk again. At the time most of the ponies were off on one of the round-ups, which indeed I had myself just left. However, my two hunting-horses, Manitou and Sorrel Joe, were at home. The former I rode myself, and on the latter I mounted one of my men who was a particularly good hand at finding and following game. With much difficulty we got together a scrub wagon team of four as unkempt, dejected, and vicious-looking broncos as ever stuck fast in a quicksand or balked in pulling up a steep pitch. Their driver was a crack whip, and their load light, consisting of little but the tent and the bedding; so we got out to the hunting-ground and back in safety; but as the river was high and the horses were weak, we came within an ace of being swamped at one crossing, and the country was so very rough that we were only able to get the wagon up the worst pitch by hauling from the saddle with the riding-animals.

We camped by an excellent spring of cold, clear water—not a common luxury in the Bad Lands. We pitched the tent beside it, getting enough timber from a grove of ash to make a large fire, which again is an appreciated blessing on the plains of the West, where we often need to carry along with us the wood for cooking our supper and breakfast, and sometimes actually have to dig up our fuel, making the fire of sage-brush roots, eked out with buffalo chips. Though the days were still warm, the nights were frosty. Our camp was in a deep valley, bounded by steep hills with sloping, grassy sides, one of them marked by a peculiar shelf of rock. The country for miles was of this same character, much broken, but everywhere passable for horsemen, and with the hills rounded and grassy, except now and then for a chain of red scoria buttes or an isolated sugar-loaf cone of gray and brown clay. The first day we spent in trying to find the probable locality of our game; and after beating pretty thoroughly over the smoother country, towards nightfall we found quite fresh elk tracks leading into a stretch of very rough and broken land about ten miles from camp.

We started next morning before the gray was relieved by the first faint flush of pink, and reached the broken country soon after sunrise. Here we dismounted and picketed our horses, as the ground we were to hunt through was very rough. Two or three hours passed before we came upon fresh signs of elk. Then we found the trails that two, from the size presumably cows, had made the preceding night, and started to follow them, carefully and noiselessly, my companion taking one side of the valley in which we were and I the other. The tracks led into one of the wildest and most desolate parts of the Bad Lands. It was now the heat of the day, the brazen sun shining out of a cloudless sky, and not the least breeze stirring. At the bottom of the valley, in the deep, narrow bed of the winding water-course, lay a few tepid little pools, almost dried up. Thick groves of stunted cedars stood here and there in the glen-like pockets of the high buttes, the peaks and sides of which were bare, and only their lower, terrace-like ledges thinly clad with coarse, withered grass and sprawling sage-brush; the parched hill-sides were riven by deep, twisted gorges, with brushwood in the bottoms; and the cliffs of coarse clay were cleft and seamed by sheer-sided, cañon-like gullies. In the narrow ravines, closed in by barren, sun-baked walls, the hot air stood still and sultry; the only living beings were the rattlesnakes, and of these I have never elsewhere seen so many. Some basked in the sun, stretched out at their ugly length of mottled brown and yellow; others lay half under stones or twined in the roots of the sage-brush, and looked straight at me with that strange, sullen, evil gaze, never shifting or moving, that is the property only of serpents and of certain men; while one or two coiled and rattled menacingly as I stepped near.

Yet, though we walked as quietly as we could, the game must have heard or smelt us; for after a mile's painstaking search we came to a dense thicket in which were two beds, evidently but just left, for the twigs and bent grass-blades were still slowly rising from the ground to which the bodies of the elk had pressed them. The long, clean hoof-prints told us that the quarry had started off at a swinging trot. We followed at once, and it was wonderful to see how such large, heavy beasts had gone up the steepest hill-sides without altering their swift and easy gait, and had plunged unhesitatingly over nearly sheer cliffs down which we had to clamber with careful slowness.

They left the strip of rugged Bad Lands and went on into the smoother country beyond, luckily passing quite close to where our horses were picketed. We thought it likely that they would halt in some heavily tim-bered coulées six or seven miles off; and as there was no need of hurry, we took lunch and then began following them up — an easy feat, as their hoofs had sunk deep into the soft soil, the prints of the dew-claws showing now and then. At first we rode, but soon dismounted, and led our horses.

We found the elk almost as soon as we struck the border of the ground we had marked as their probable halting-place. Our horses were unshod, and made but little noise; and coming to a wide, long coulée filled with tall trees and brushwood, we as usual separated, I going down one side and my companion the other. When nearly half-way down he suddenly whistled sharply, and I of course at once stood still, with my rifle at the ready. Nothing moved, and I glanced at him. He had squatted down and was gazing earnestly over into the dense laurel on my side of the coulée. In a minute he shouted that he saw a red patch in the brush which he thought must be the elk, and that it was right between him and myself. Elk will sometimes lie as closely as rabbits, even when not in very good cover; still I was a little surprised at these not breaking out when they heard human voices. However, there they staid; and I waited several minutes in vain for them to move. From where I stood it was impossible to see them, and I was fearful that they might go off down the valley and so offer me a very poor shot. Meanwhile, Manitou, who is not an emotional horse, and is moreover blessed with a large appetite, was feed-ing greedily, rattling his bridle-chains at every mouthful; and I thought that he would act as a guard to keep the elk where they were until I shifted my position. So I slipped back, and ran swiftly round the head of the coulée to where my companion was still sitting. He pointed me out the patch of red in the bushes, not sixty yards distant, and I fired into it without delay, by good luck breaking the neck of a cow elk, when immediately another one rose up from beside it and made off. I had five shots at her as she ascended the hill-side and the gentle slope beyond; and two of my bullets struck her close together in the flank, ranging forward — a very fatal shot. She was evidently mortally hit, and just as she reached the top of the divide she stopped, reeled, and fell over, dead.

We were much pleased with our luck, as it secured us an ample stock of needed fresh meat; and the two elk lay very handily, so that on the following day we were able to stop for them with the wagon on our way homeward, putting them in bodily, and leaving only the entrails for the vultures that were already soaring in great circles over the carcasses.*

Much the finest elk antlers I ever got, as a trophy of my own rifle, were from a mighty bull that I killed far to the west of my ranch, in the eastern chains of the Rockies. I shot him early one morning, while still-hunting through the open glades of a great pine forest, where the frosty dew was still heavy on the grass. We had listened to him and his fellows challenging each other all night long. Near by the call of the bulls in the rutting season—their "whistling," as the frontiersmen term it—sounds harsh and grating; but heard in the depths of their own mountain fastnesses, ringing through the frosty night, and echoing across the ravines and under the silent archways of the pines, it has a grand, musical beauty of its own that makes it, to me, one of the most attractive sounds in nature.

At this season the bulls fight most desperately, and their combats are far more often attended with fatal results than is the case with deer. In the grove back of my ranch house, when we first took possession, we found the skulls of two elk with interlocked antlers; one was a royal, the other had fourteen points. Theirs had been a duel to the death.

In hunting, whether on the prairie or in the deep woods, a man ought to pay great heed to his surroundings, so as not to get lost. To an old hand, getting lost is not so very serious; because, if he has his rifle and some matches, and does not lose his head, the worst that can happen to him is having to suffer some temporary discomfort. But a novice is in imminent danger of losing his wits, and therefore his life. To a man

---

* No naturalist ever described the way vultures gather with more scientific accuracy than Longfellow:

> "Never stoops the soaring vulture
> On his quarry in the desert,
> On the sick or wounded bison,
> But another vulture, watching
> From his high aërial lookout,
> Sees the downward plunge, and follows;
> And a third pursues the second,
> Coming from the invisible ether,
> First a speck, and then a vulture,
> Till the air is dark with pinions."

totally unaccustomed to it the sense of utter loneliness is absolutely appalling: the feeling of being lost in the wilderness seems to drive him into a state of panic terror that is frightful to behold, and that in the end renders him bereft of reason. When he realizes that he is lost he often will begin to travel very fast, and finally run until he falls exhausted—only to rise again and repeat the process when he has recovered his strength. If not found in three or four days, he is very apt to become crazy; he will then flee from the rescuers, and must be pursued and captured as if he were a wild animal.

Since 1884, when I went to the Big Horn Mountains, I have killed no grizzlies. There are some still left in our neighborhood, but they are very shy, and live in such inaccessible places, that, though I have twice devoted several days solely to hunting them, I was unsuccessful each time. A year ago, however, two cowboys found a bear in the open, and after the expenditure of a great number of cartridges killed it with their revolvers, the bear charging gamely to the last.

But this feat sinks into insignificance when compared with the deed of General W. H. Jackson, of Bellemeade, Tennessee, who is probably the only man living who ever, single-handed, killed a grizzly bear with a cavalry saber. It was many years ago, when he was a young officer in the United States service. He was with a column of eight companies of mounted infantry under the command of Colonel Andrew Porter, when by accident a bear was roused and lumbered off in front of them. Putting spurs to his thoroughbred, he followed the bear, and killed it with the saber, in sight of the whole command.

HERALDING THE SUNRISE.

THE BIG-HORN SHEEP

A MOUNTAIN HUNTER.

XI

The Big-Horn Sheep

IT has happened that I have generally hunted big-horn during weather of arctic severity; so that in my mind this great sheep is inseparably associated with snow-clad, desolate wastes, ice-coated crags, and the bitter cold of a northern winter; whereas the sight of a prong-buck, the game that we usually hunt early in the season, always recalls to me the endless green of the midsummer prairies as they shimmer in the sunlight.

Yet in reality the big-horn is by no means confined to any one climatic zone. Along the interminable mountain chains of the Great Divide it ranges south to the hot, dry table-lands of middle Mexico, as well as far to the northward of the Canadian boundary, among the towering and tremendous peaks where the glaciers are fed from fields of everlasting snow. There exists no animal more hardy, nor any better fitted to grapple with the extremes of heat and cold. Droughts, scanty pasturage, or deep snows make it shift its ground, but never mere variation of temperature. The lofty mountains form its favorite abode, but it is almost equally at home in any large tract of very rough and broken ground. It is by no means an exclusively alpine animal, like the white goat. It is not only found throughout the main chains of the Rockies, as well as on the Sierras of the south and the coast ranges of western Oregon, Washington, and British Columbia, but it also exists to the east among the clusters of high hills and the stretches of barren Bad Lands that break the monotonous level of the great plains.

Throughout most of its range the big-horn is a partly migratory beast. In the summer it seeks the highest mountains, often passing above timber-line; and when the fall snows deepen it comes down to the lower spurs or foot-hills, or may even travel some distance southward. If there is a large tract of Bad Lands near the mountains, sheep may be plentiful in them throughout the severe weather, while in the summer not a single individual will be found in its winter haunts, all having then retired to the high peaks.

Sometimes big-horn wander widely for reasons unconnected with the weather: all of those in a district may suddenly leave it and perhaps not return for several years. Such is often the result of a district being settled, or being exposed to incessant hunting. After a certain number of sheep have been killed the remainder may all disappear, possibly one or two small bands only staying behind; but it is quite likely that two or three years later the bulk of the vanished host will come back again.

But where the region that they inhabit is cut off from the mountains by settled districts, or by great stretches of plain and prairie, then the sheep that dwell therein can make no such migrations. Thus they live all the year round in the Little Missouri Bad Lands; and though the different bands wander away and to and fro for scores of miles, especially in the fall,— for big-horn are far more restless than deer,— yet they do not shift their positions much on account of the season, and are often found in precisely the same places both summer and winter. They thus bear with indifference exposure to the extremes of heat and cold in a climate where the yearly variation reaches the utmost possible limit, the thermometer sometimes covering a range of a hundred and seventy degrees in the course of twelve months. There are few spots on earth much hotter than these Bad Lands during a spell of fierce summer weather, and, unlike the deer, the sheep cannot seek the shade of the dense thickets. In the glare of midday the naked angular hills yield no shelter whatever; the barren ravines between them turn into ovens beneath the brazen sun. The still, lifeless, burning air stifles those who breathe it, while the parched and heat-cracked cañon walls are intolerable to the touch.

But though the mountain sheep can stand this, and in fact do so with even less protection than the deer, yet they certainly dislike it more than do the latter. If mountains are near, they go up them far sooner and far higher than the deer. On the other hand, they bear the winter blizzards much better, caring less for shelter, and keeping their strength pretty well. Ordinarily when in the Bad Lands they do not shift their ground save to get on the lee side of the cliffs, though the deep snows of course drive them from the mountains. A very heavy fall of snow, if they are high up on the hills, occasionally forces a band to enter the evergreen woods and make a regular yard, as deer do, beneath the overhanging cover-giving branches; then they subsist on the scanty browse until they can get back to pasture lands. But this is rare. Generally they stay in the open, and bid defiance to the elements; yet, like other game, they often seem to have the knack of foretelling any storm or cold spell of unusual severity and length.   On the eve of such a storm they frequently retreat to some secure haven of refuge.   This may be a nook or cranny in the rocks, or merely a slight hollow to leeward of a little grove of stunted pines; and there the band may have to stay without food for several days, until the storm is over. Occasionally they succumb to the deep snow; but if they have any kind of chance for their lives, this happens less often than with either deer or antelope.

The big-horn, or cimarrón sheep, as the Mexicans call it, is the sole American representative of the different kinds of mountain sheep that are found in the Old World.   It is fourfold the weight of the Mediterranean moufflon.   Its nearest relative, from which it is with difficulty distinguished, is the huge argali, three or four varieties — some say species — of which are to be found in the high lands of central Asia.   The American and Asiatic animals seem to grade into one another as regards size; the north Asiatic argali is said to be no larger than the big-horn, but the giant Himalayan sheep, or nyan, averages heavier, both in body and horns, and especially in length of legs.   The horns of the argali have more outward twist.   The largest big-horn of which I have ever been able to get authentic record was one killed in Montana by a ranch friend of mine, and carefully weighed and measured at the time.   At the shoulder he stood just three feet eight inches; he weighed very nearly four hundred pounds; and his single unbroken horn was in girth nineteen inches, and in length along the curve forty-two.   But such a ram is a giant.   The largest I have myself shot I had no means of weighing: it was just after the rutting season, and he was as gaunt as a greyhound.   At the shoulder he stood three feet five inches; and his horns, which were thick for their length, were in girth sixteen and a half inches, and in length thirty.   The nyan of Thibet, on the other hand, stands four feet high; and exceptional rams have horns twenty-three inches round the base and upwards of fifty in length, while the average full-grown one will perhaps have them seventeen inches by thirty-eight.   The nyan thus certainly stands before the big-horn, although even among full-grown animals many heads of the latter would be above the average of the former.   The difference in the habits of the two animals is very marked, for according to the English sportsmen the nyan keeps exclusively to the high, open plains, or barren, gently sloping hills; whereas the big-horn, like the Old World ibex, is a beast of the crags and precipices, and though sometimes venturing into the level country, yet at the first alarm it invariably dashes for the broken ground.

Our American mountain sheep usually go in bands of from fifteen to thirty individuals, occasionally of many more; while often small parties of two or three will stay by themselves.   In the winter, or sometimes not until the early spring, the old rams separate.   The oldest and finest are often found entirely alone, retiring to the most inaccessible solitudes; the younger ones keep in little flocks of perhaps half a dozen or so.   The main band then consists only of the ewes, the yearlings, and now and then a two-year-old; and this also is soon broken up, leaving merely the yearlings and the barren ewes, for about the middle of May the ewes that are heavy with young leave the rest, each by herself.   Like the old rams, they now seek the most inaccessible and far-off places—high up the mountains, if possible; otherwise, in the barren and unfrequented portions of the Bad Lands, where the steep hills and abrupt valleys are twisted into a mere tangle of precipitous crests and cañons.   Here the ewe makes her lying-in bed—oval in shape, like that of a prong-horn or black-tail doe, but made by pawing out, or perhaps merely wearing out, a slight hollow in the bare soil; whereas the doe crushes down with her weight the long grass of the prairie or thicket.   This bed is usually made on the ledge of a cliff, on the side where there is most shelter from the prevailing winds; perhaps it is beneath a great rock or clay bowlder, with not so much as a blade of grass around, or it may be partly screened by a few wind-beaten sage-bushes.   Generally only one, but sometimes two, young are brought forth at a birth.   The young lamb matches his surroundings wonderfully in color, and the ewe is very careful in going to him to be sure that she is unobserved.   For the first day or two the lamb trusts for his safety solely to not being seen by the beasts and birds of prey.   He crouches flat down, like an antelope fawn, and it is next to impossible for human eyes to discover him save by accident.   Once only I stumbled across a newly born lamb.   It was about the first of June, and I found him lying by the bed of the mother as I was going along a ledge, scantily covered with sage brush, in the heart of some high, wild hills, about fifteen miles from my ranch.   The little fellow was too young to show much alarm when I handled and petted him and with much difficulty persuaded him to stand up on his helplessly weak and awkward little legs.   The mother was about two hundred yards distant, and was greatly frightened when I drew near her offspring; she hung about in the distance for a short time and then dashed off.   However, she must have returned when I left; for two or three days later, when from curiosity I came back, the little fellow was gone.

When the young are able to clamber about for short distances almost as well as the old, then the nursing ewes and their lambs rejoin the band, some time in July. The band now keeps in the neighborhood of water and where the feed is good — comparatively good, at least, for the scanty pasturage that grows on the mountains and barren hills haunted by the sheep would hardly please more luxury-loving animals. The flocks of ewes and lambs are at this time quite easily discovered, but of course no man but a game butcher would dream of molesting them. In September the young rams begin to join them, and soon afterwards the old patriarchs likewise come down from their remote fastnesses.

The rams now fight desperately among themselves for the possession of the ewes, rushing together with a shock that would shatter their skulls were they less strong; while the battered horns, with splintered ends, bear witness to the violence of the contests. These contests are free from one danger, however; the horns do not get interlocked, and thus cause the death of both combatants. This is not only a common accident among deer and elk, but it even happens to antelope; I knew of one instance where two prong-horn bucks, who had evidently been battling for a doe, were found dead, side by side, partly eaten by the coyotes. The right horn of one and the left horn of the other had become locked together so firmly, thanks to the prong and the hook at the end, that they could not be drawn apart, and the two beasts had died miserably in con-sequence. Each herd has some acknowledged master ram, but he may tolerate the presence of three or four others of lesser degree, together with the ewes, lambs, and yearlings that go to make up the rest of the flock; or else, if a cross old fellow, the master ram may turn out all the others, or may content himself with a little bunch of merely three or four ewes. So that even at this season several young rams may be found by themselves; or a morose old veteran, time-worn and battle-scarred, may keep entirely alone. As soon as the rutting season is over many of these exiles rejoin the band; and at this time, when the rams are of course in very poor condition, they are all apt to come down on the levels more boldly than at any other season, to get at the good grass, although even now rarely venturing very far from the hills. While thus on the edges of the plains, their natural wariness seems to increase tenfold.

But at all times their habits are very variable; for they are restless, wandering beasts, with something whimsical in their tempers, and given at times to queer freaks. If the fit seize them, and especially if they have been alarmed or annoyed, they may at any time leave their accustomed dwelling-places, or act in a manner absolutely contrary to their usual conduct. About noon one hot midsummer day, three great rams crossed

the river just below our ranch, stopping to drink, and spending some time
on the sand-bars, occasionally playfully butting at each other. They
trotted off before they could be stalked.   To get down to the river they
had to pass over a level plain half a mile wide; and once across, they went
through a dense wood choked with underbrush for nearly half a mile
more before again coming to the steep bluffs.   On another occasion, in
the rutting season, one of my cowboys encountered a mountain-ram crossing a broad, level river-bottom at midday.   Occasionally a ram will join a
flock of ewes, or a ewe and a yearling, in the spring.   Two or three times
I have known them to come boldly up to the bluffs that overlook and
skirt a little frontier town, and there to stay grazing or resting for several
hours; but they always made off in plenty of time to avoid the hunters
who finally went after them.   Once I shot one within a few hundred yards
of my ranch house.   I was returning home, weary and unsuccessful, after
a long day's tramp over hills where black-tail usually were common.
When nearly home I struck into a well-beaten cattle-trail, leading down
a deep, narrow ravine which cleft in two a knot of jagged hills; it was a
favorite range for our horses, and so was frequently ridden over by the
cowboys.   On turning round a corner of the ravine, a sudden snort to one
side and above me made me hastily look up, shifting my rifle from my
shoulder.   On my right the sheer wall of clay rose up without a break for
perhaps two hundred feet or so, its thin, notched crest showing against
the sky-line as sharply as if cut with a knife; and on a little jutting pinnacle was perched a mountain sheep, its four hoofs all together on a space
no larger than the palms of a man's hands.   It was facing me and staring
down at me, so that the bullet went right into its chest, splitting its heart
fairly open.   Yet it did not fall forward over the cliff, but wheeled on its
haunches and went along the crest at a mad, plunging gallop, finally
crossing out of sight.   Almost as soon as it disappeared a column of
dust rose from the other side of the ridge, making me think that it had
fallen some distance, striking hard on the dry clay.   The guess was a
good one, and when, after a long circle and some climbing, I reached the
spot, I found a fine young barren ewe lying dead at the foot of a high
cut bank.

But all such instances as these are wholly exceptional, and are chiefly
interesting as showing that mountain sheep act more erratically and less
according to rule than do most other kinds of game.   They seem to have
fits of restless waywardness, or even of panic curiosity; and so at times
wander into unlooked-for places, or betray a sudden heedlessness of dan-
gers against which they on ordinary occasions carefully guard.   This last

freak, however, is generally shown only in very wild localities or among young animals. Where hunters are scarce or almost unknown, all wild animals are very bold. I have seen deer in remote forests, and even in little-hunted localities near my ranch, so tame that they would stand looking at the hunter within fifty yards for several minutes before taking flight. Mountain sheep under similar circumstances show a lordly disregard for the human intruder, leaving his presence at a leisurely gait, in strong contrast to the mad gallop of their more sophisticated brethren when alarmed.

In fact, much of the wariness among beasts of chase, as well as much of the courage shown by the more ferocious, depends upon the degree in which they have been harried by hunters, although much also depends upon the character of the species. European game is thus generally wilder than American; but no animal could be more difficult to approach than a Maine moose. The deer of the Adirondacks and Alleghanies are almost as wary, and in those parts of the Rockies where they have been much molested, big-horn are as shy as the chamois of the Alps, or the ibex of the Pyrenees. So the sloth bear and leopard of India are now much more vicious and dangerous to man than are the black bear and cougar of the United States, simply because of the different race of human beings by whom they are surrounded.

No animal seems to have been more changed by domestication than the sheep. The timid, helpless, fleecy idiot of the folds, the most foolish of all tame animals, has hardly a trait in common with his self-reliant wild relative who combines the horns of a sheep with the hide of a deer, whose home is in the rocks and the mountains, and who is so abundantly able to take care of himself. Wild sheep are as good mountaineers as wild goats, or as mountain antelopes, and are to the full as wary and intelligent.

A very short experience with the rifle-bearing portion of mankind changes the big-horn into a quarry whose successful chase taxes to the utmost the skill alike of still-hunter and of mountaineer. A solitary old ram seems to be ever on the watch. His favorite resting-place is a shelf or terrace-end high up on some cliff, from whence he can see far and wide over the country round about. The least sound—the rattle of a loose stone, a cough, even a heavy footfall on hard earth—attracts his attention, making him at once clamber up on some peak to try for a glimpse of the danger. His eyes catch the slightest movement. His nose is as keen as an elk's, and gives him surer warning than any other sense; the slightest taint in the air produces immediate flight in the direction away from the danger. But there is one compensation, from the hunter's standpoint, for his wonderfully developed smelling powers; he lives in such very broken country that the currents of air often go over his head, so that it is at times possible to hunt him almost down wind.

A band of sheep is, if anything, even more difficult to approach than is a single ram; but, on the other hand, it is far easier to get on the track of and to find out, as there are always some young members guilty of indiscretions. All of the flock are ever on the lookout. While the others are grazing there is always at least one with its head up; and occasionally a particularly watchful ewe will jump up on some bowlder, or at least stand with her fore-legs against its side, so as to get a wider view. Any unexplained sight or sound is announced to the rest of the herd by a kind of hissing snort, or sometimes by a stamp of the forefoot on the ground. If the intruder is either smelt or seen, the whole herd instantly break into the strong but not particularly swift gallop which distinguishes the species, and go straight away from the danger towards the roughest ground that they can reach. If, however, only alarmed by a sound, or if the suspicious object is some distance off, the animals often run together into a bunch and stand gazing in its direction for a few seconds prior to making off. Among cliffs and precipices the echoes are so confusing that if the hunter keeps out of sight the herd occasionally become utterly bewildered by the firing, and, as a result, spend several fatal minutes in a futile running to and fro, uncertain what course will take them out of danger. One day my cousin, West Roosevelt, after a long and careful stalk, got close up to three sheep in a very deep and narrow ravine; and although, owing to their being almost underneath him, he at first overshot, yet all three of the startled and panic-struck animals were killed before they recovered their wits sufficiently to run out of range.

But a chance like this may not happen once in a hunter's lifetime. Of all American game, this is the one in whose pursuit the successful hunter needs to show most skill, hardihood, and resolution. On ordinary occasions a big-horn, when menaced by danger, flees beyond its reach with instant decision and headlong speed, disappearing with incredible rapidity over ground where it needs an expert cragsman to so much as follow at a walk. Its wonderful feats of climbing have, as with the chamois and ibex of the Old World, given rise to many fables, the most widespread being the belief that the rams, in plunging down precipices, alight on their horns. So the chamois was said to hang over ledges by means of its short, hooked horns, and when cornered on the edge of a sheer precipice, where there was no escape from the hunter, of its own accord to thrust its body against his outstretched knife—as we read and see pictured in the German hunting-books of two or three centuries ago, such as the quaint old "Adeliche Weidwerke."

The mountain sheep of America, when the choice is open to them,

SHOT!

actually seem to prefer regions as wild and rugged as they are sterile. The tufts of grass between the rocks, the scanty blades that grow on the clay buttes, suffice for their wants, and the amount of climbing necessary to get at them is literally a matter of indifference to beasts whose muscles are like whipcord and whose tendons are like steel. A big-horn is a marvelous leaper, perhaps even better when the jump is perpendicular than when it is horizontal. His poise is perfect; his eye and foot work together with unerring accuracy. One will unhesitatingly bound or drop a dozen feet on to a little rock pinnacle where there is scarce a hand's breadth on which to stand. The presence of the tiniest cracks in the otherwise smooth surface of a sheer rock wall enables a mountain sheep to go up it with ease. The proud, lordly bearing of an old ram makes him look exactly what he is, one of the noblest of game animals; his port is the same whether at rest or in motion. Except when very badly frightened, his movements are all made with a certain self-confident absence of hurry, as if he were conscious of a vast reserve power of strength and activity on which to draw at need. As a mountaineer he is the embodi-

25

ment of elastic, sinewy strength and self-command rather than of mere nervous agility.   He hardly ever makes a mistake, even when rushing at speed over the slippery, ice-coated crags in winter.

The most difficult of all climbing is to go over rocks when the ice has filled up all the chinks and crannies, and the flat slabs are glassy in their hard smoothness.   A black-tail buck is no mean climber; yet under such circumstances I have seen one lose his footing and tumble head over heels, scraping great handfuls of hair off his hide; but I have never known a big-horn to make a misstep.   This is undoubtedly largely owing to the difference between the two animals in the structure of their feet. A sheep's hoof is an elastic pad, only the rims and the toe-points being hard, and it thus gets a good grip on the slightest projection, or on any little roughness in the rock.   The tracks are very different from deer tracks, being nearly square in form, instead of heart-shaped, the prints of the toes rather deep and wide apart, even when the animal has been walking.

A band of sheep will often seem to court certain death by plunging off the brink of what looks like a perpendicular cliff, where there is not a ledge or a crack yielding foot-hold.   In such cases, if the cliff is high, it will be found on examination that it is not quite perpendicular, and that the sheep, in making the fearful descent, from time to time touch or strike the cliff with their hoofs, thus going down in long bounds, keeping their poise all the time.   The final bound is often made almost head first, as if they were diving.

Narrow ledges, overlooking an abyss the fathomless depths of which would make even a trained cragsman giddy, are very favorite resorts. So are the crests of the ridges themselves.   If in any patch of Bad Lands there is an unusually high chain of steep, bare clay buttes, mountain sheep are sure to select their tops as a regular parade-ground.   After a rain the clay takes their hoof-prints as clearly as if it were sealing-wax, and all along the top of the crest they beat out a regular walk from one end to the other, with occasional little side-paths leading out to some overhanging shoulder or jutting spur, from whence there is a good view of the surrounding country.

Generally the band is led by a ewe; but in a case of immediate and pressing danger the ram assumes the headship.   Aside from man, mountain sheep have fewer foes than most other game.   Bears are too clumsy to catch them; and lynx and fox, inveterate enemies of fawns, rarely get up to the high, breezy nurseries of the young lambs.   Wolves and cougars, however, harass them greatly.   A wolf will not attack an old ram if he can help it, but sneaks after the ewes and lambs, waiting until they get on somewhat level ground, and then running one down by sheer speed before it can take refuge among the secure fastnesses of the precipices.

The cougar relies on stealth, not on speed, and gets his game either by fair stalking or else by lying in wait. Sometimes he can creep up to a band while they are taking their siesta; but generally they keep too sharp a lookout, and he has to approach them while they are feeding, or when they have come down to drink. Some fifteen miles from my ranch is a tract of very rough country, the sides of the hills falling off into precipices or into dark, cedar-clad gorges. This was a favorite resort of mountain sheep; but one spring a couple of cougars took up their abode in the neighborhood, and soon killed several of the sheep and drove the others away. Judging by the tracks and by the position of the carcasses, they must have done the killing in the morning and evening, creeping up to the doomed animals as they fed on the lower slopes, or lurking round the spring-holes and little alkali pools where they drank. The great war eagle is one of the worst enemies of the young lambs.

In the rutting season a ram will make a good fight if he has any chance at all, and at that time is very bold and pugnacious. If followed by a dog he will frequently decline to run, turning to bay at once. One hunter whom I knew killed several in this way by the aid of a collie. Of course it cannot be done when once the sheep have begun to realize that the dog is merely an ally of the man, for they then look out for the latter.

Sheep are easily tamed, if taken young, and make amusing pets. A friend in Helena, Montana, once owned a tame ram. When young he was a great favorite. He was an inquisitive, mischievous creature, of marvelous activity. It was impossible to keep him out of the garden. A single hop would carry him over the high fence; if an inmate of the house came to the rescue, another hop carried the intruder once more into outside safety, and a third took him back again the second the rescuer had turned around. Whenever he got the chance he would pull down the clothes that had been hung up to dry. When he could get inside the house he was fond of walking on the mantel-piece. He was the terror of the Chinese cook, whom he soon discovered to be afraid of him, and would lie in wait outside the kitchen door so as to butt him when he appeared. This was at first done in mere playfulness; but as he grew older he became morose and quarrelsome, and had to be disposed of.

It is impossible to hunt big-horn successfully without some knowledge of their habits. They go down to drink in the very late evening, or sometimes in the gray of the morning; when the moon is full they may not go to the water until long after nightfall. Generally they drink later than any other game; but all game vary their habits now and then in this regard. The prong-buck, though diurnal, sometimes comes to a watering-hole during the night; and I have once or twice seen both deer and sheep drinking at midday.

In ordinary weather they begin to feed early in the morning, and when the sun has risen some little distance above the horizon they start to graze their way slowly up to the high spur or ridge crest where they intend to lie during the day. Here they stay until well on in the afternoon, and then again descend to their feeding-grounds on the lower slopes. In very cold weather, however, they are apt to be found grazing at midday. A raging snow blizzard may keep them lying close under cover for three days at a time: they naturally get ravenous, and when there is a lull, or especially if it is succeeded by a short spell of good weather, they come hastily out to feed, no matter what the time of day may be.

As with almost all game except antelope, they can be best hunted in the morning and evening; but, unlike deer, they can also be followed throughout the day, for whereas elk, black-tail, and white-tail have then all alike retired to the thickets, the big-horn take their noontide rest lying out in plain view. If the hunter means to catch them feeding he should make a very early start. A good pair of field-glasses is of great service, for the two essential requisites to success are the capacity to take long walks over rough ground and painstaking care in scanning the country far and wide, so as to see the game before it sees the hunter. There is then a chance to stalk up close, the broken ground frequently yielding good cover.

Often it may be necessary to lie for hours carefully concealed, watching a flock that is in an unfavorable position, and waiting until it shifts its ground. This is not very comfortable on a cold day in November or December, the months in which I have usually hunted big-horn, devoting the early fall to the chase of elk and deer. But it is often the only way to secure success: patience and perseverance are two of the still-hunter's cardinal virtues. Personally I have always owed whatever success I have had to dogged perseverance and patient persistence, and on a lamentably large number of occasions have had to draw heavily on these qualities to make good a lack of skill, sometimes with the rifle, sometimes in mountaineering. Among many hunting trips I can recall not a few where willingness to lie still two or three hours under trying circumstances in the end got me the game; and one such instance may serve as a sample of the rest.

I was staying at the line camp of two of my cowboys, a small dug-out in the side of a butte that marked the edge of the Bad Lands, the rolling prairie coming up to its base. The quarters were cramped for three men, an entire side of the little hut being filled by the two bunks in which we slept,— I in the upper, my two companions in the lower,— while the fire-place occupied one end, the mess-box served as a table, and the earth-covered roof of logs was so low that we could hardly stand upright. Win-dow there was none; but it was snug, and, for a line camp, clean. There was plenty of fire-wood, and, for a wonder, the chimney did not smoke; so we were comfortable enough. The butte itself served for three out of the four walls. No other building is so warm as a dug-out, and in the terrible winter weather of Dakota and Montana warmth is the one thing for which all else must be sacrificed.*

In such high latitudes the December sun rises late. Long before day-break we had finished our breakfast of bread, beans, and coffee. The two cowboys had saddled their shaggy ponies—which had spent the night in the rough log stable — and had ridden off in opposite directions along their lonely beat, muffled in their wolf-skin overcoats and heavy shaps; while I strode off on foot towards the high hills that lay riverward, my rifle on my shoulder and my fur cap pulled down well over my ears.

The cold was biting, for even at noon the sun had not power to thaw the frozen ground. But there was very little snow; just enough to powder the hills and to lie in patches in the hollows. I walked rapidly up a long coulée, then climbed up a steep rounded hill and followed the divide back into the heart of the Bad Lands. By the time I was on my chosen hunting-grounds the sun had topped the horizon behind me, and his level rays lit up the peaks and crests.

The next hour was spent in hard climbing and incessant watchfulness. The hills lay in isolated masses. I clambered painfully up their slippery sides, creeping along the narrow icy ledges that ran across the faces of the cliffs, and cautiously working my way over the smooth shoulders. From behind every ridge and spur I carefully examined the opposite hill-sides, using the field-glasses if there was scope for them. Sheep, standing still or lying down, are often very hard to see, their coats assimilating curiously with the neutral-tinted cliffs and bowlders; but against snow they of course stand out much more distinctly.

At last, as I lay peeping over the ragged crest of a clay butte, I made out a small dark object half way up a steep slope some six hundred yards

---

* I have camped out when the thermometer showed 65 degrees of frost; *not* —65°, as I see I once put it by a mistake in copying my rough field-notes.

down the valley; and another look showed me that it was a ram feeding leisurely up the hill-side. The wind was good for a direct approach. I got off the butte by carefully letting myself down from one little ledge or niche to another, and started along the valley towards the ram, only to find my way barred by a deep chasm whose straight, ice-coated sides yawned too far apart to permit of any attempt at crossing. There was no help for it but laboriously to retrace my steps and make my way round its head with what speed I could. This I did, the work making me thoroughly warm for the first time that morning. Once across the walking was better, and I went down the valley-side at a good pace, until I came to a shoulder some two hundred yards from where I had seen the sheep. I was a good deal higher than where he had stood; but in the time I had been out of sight of him he must have gone up the hill quite a distance, for when I looked round the shoulder I saw him about as far off as I expected, but above instead of below me. Slow though my movements had been when I cautiously looked round the edge, they had not escaped his quick eye; for when I made him out he was standing motionless, gazing in my direction. Before I could raise my rifle he gave a great jump sideways and galloped off, disappearing instantly behind a huge mass of detached sandstone, and I never saw him again.

A little chagrined at my fruitless stalk I plodded on, doing much hard climbing but seeing no signs of game until nearly midday. Then in the snow at the head of a coulée I came across the tracks of a band evidently made that morning while returning from the feeding-grounds. I followed them until I became convinced that the animals had gone to a great table-land or plateau that I could see a good way ahead; then, as the wind was behind me, I struck off to one side, made a circle through some very rough country, and clambered out along the knife-like crests of a line of high hills separated from the plateau by a broad valley. Every hundred paces or so I would stop and examine the country far and near with the glasses; often I had to crawl on all-fours to avoid appearing against the sky-line on the ridge.

At last I caught sight of the band. There were some fifteen or twenty of them, and they were lying at the point of a spur that was thrust out from the plateau, nearly opposite to me and half a mile off. They were in a position which it was impossible to approach within six hundred yards without being observed, for they could see over the level plateau behind them, and from the brink of the lofty cliff on which they lay they looked up, down, and across the wild, deep valley beneath.

With the glasses I could make out that there was no good head among them; but I was out for meat rather than for sport. They were very watchful, ever on the lookout; and as the afternoon wore on one of the more restless would now and then get up, walk off a few steps, or stand gazing intently into the far distance. There was nothing for me to do except to wait until they grew hungry and shifted their position to some place which there was a chance of my approaching unseen. So for three hours I lay on the iron ground, under the lee of a bowlder that but partly shielded me from the wind, munching the strip of jerked venison I had carried in my pocket, and peeping at the sheep through a tuft of tall, coarse grass that grew on top of the ridge.

At last, when it wanted but little more than an hour of sunset, the sheep all got on their legs, one after another, and, led by an old ewe, began to descend into the valley. They went down the cliff by a sort of break or slide, hopping dexterously from rock to rock. On coming to the steep slope at its foot they struck into a trot, which merged into a fast gallop as they got nearly down. I feared that they would stop before coming to the cañon at the bottom of the valley; but they did not, crossing it without hesitation, for all its sheer-sided and slippery depth, and continuing their course towards the end of the chain of hills on which I was, where they halted to graze, after going up nearly to the top. It was excellent ground for a stalk. The ridge went down to the left in the steep, grassy slopes on which they were feeding, while on the right it broke abruptly off into a precipice, with a narrow ledge high up along its face.

This ledge made the approach an easy one. The only difficult places were those where the ledge was interrupted, and I had either cautiously to make my way along the face of the cliff,— a very unpleasant task, as the slight hollows or knobs which served me as foot-holds were slippery with ice, the risk of a fall being thus enormously increased,— or else was forced to go to the top, and, sprawling flat on the smooth slope, drag myself along just to one side of the ridge. I had marked the position of the game by a dwarfed cedar that grew in a crevice on the very crest. It gave excellent cover, and on reaching it and peering out through the branches, I saw the sheep scattered out only some sixty yards below me, and, choosing out a fine young ram, I fired, breaking both shoulders. They all rushed together, and then without an instant's pause raced madly down the hill-side, neither of the two bullets that I sent after them taking effect. I had no time to lose; so I dressed the ram hastily, tilted him up so that the blood would run out, and left him to be called for with the pony next day. Then I made the best use of the waning light to get to a long divide, furrowed by many buffalo trails, which I knew I could follow even when it grew dark, and which came out on the prairie not very far to one side of the line camp.

The day on which I was lucky enough to shoot my largest and finest ram was memorable in more ways than one. The shot was one of the best I ever made,—albeit the element of chance doubtless entered into it far more largely than the element of skill,—and in coming home from the hunt I got quite badly frozen.

The day before we had come back from a week's trip after deer; for we were laying in the winter stock of meat. We had been camped far down the river, and had intended to take two days on the return trip, as the wagon was rather heavily loaded, for we had killed eight deer. The morning we broke camp was so mild that I did not put on my heaviest winter clothing, starting off in the same that I had worn during the past few days' still-hunting among the hills. Before we had been gone an hour, however, the sky grew overcast and the wind began to blow from the north with constantly increasing vigor. The sky grew steadily more gloomy and lowering, the gusts came ever harder and harder, and by noon the winter day had darkened and a furious gale was driving against us. The blasts almost swept me from my saddle and the teamster from his seat, while we were glad to wrap ourselves in our huge fur coats to keep out the growing cold. Soon after midday the wagon suddenly broke down while we were yet in mid-prairie. It was evident that we were on the eve of a furious snow-blizzard, which might last a few hours, or else, perhaps, as many days. We were miles from any shelter that would permit us to light a fire in the face of such a storm; so we left the wagon as it was, hastily unharnessed the team horses, and, with the driver riding one and leading the other, struck off homeward at a steady gallop. Once fairly caught by the blizzard in a country that we only partly knew, it would have been hopeless to do more than to try for some ravine in which to cower till it was over; so we pushed our horses to their utmost pace. Our object was to reach the head coulées of a creek leading down to the river but a few miles from the ranch. Could we get into these before the snow struck us we felt we would be all right, for we could then find our way home, even in pitch-darkness, with the wind in the quarter from which it was coming. So, with the storm on our backs, we rode at full speed through the gathering gloom, across the desolate reaches of prairie. The tough little horses, instead of faltering, went stronger mile by mile. At last the weird rows of hills loomed vaguely up in our front, and we plunged into the deep ravines for which we had been heading just as the whirling white wreaths struck us—not the soft, feathery flakes of a sea-board snow-storm, but fine ice-dust, driven level by the wind, choking us, blinding our eyes, and cutting our faces if we turned towards it. The roar of the blizzard drowned our voices when we were but six feet apart: had it not been on our backs we could not have gone a hundred yards, for we could no more face it than we could face a frozen sand-blast. In an instant the strange, wild outlines of the high buttes between which we were riding were shrouded from our sight. We had to grope our way through a kind of shimmering dusk; and when once or twice we were obliged by some impassable cliff or cañon to retrace our steps, it was all that we could do to urge the horses even a few paces against the wind-blown snow-grains which stung like steel filings. But this extreme violence only lasted about four hours. The moon was full, and its beams struggled through scudding clouds and snow-drift, so that we reached the ranch without difficulty, and when we got there the wind had already begun to lull. The snow still fell thick and fast; but before we went to bed this also showed signs of stopping. Accordingly we determined that we would leave the wagon where it was for a day or two, and start early next morning for a range of high hills some ten miles off, much haunted by sheep; for we did not wish to let pass the chance of tracking the game offered by the first good snow of the season.

Next morning we started by starlight. The snow lay several inches deep on the ground; the whole land was a dazzling white. It was very cold. Within the ranch everything was frozen solid in spite of the thick log walls; but the air was so still and clear that we did not realize how low the temperature was. Accordingly, as the fresh horse I had to take was young and wild, I did not attempt to wear my fur coat. I soon felt my mistake. The windless cold ate into my marrow; and when, shortly after the cloudless winter sunrise, we reached our hunting-grounds and picketed out the horses, I was already slightly frost-bitten. But the toil of hunting over the snow-covered crags soon made me warm.

All day we walked and climbed through a white wonderland. On every side the snowy hills, piled one on another, stretched away, chain after chain, as far as sight could reach. The stern and iron-bound land had been changed to a frozen sea of billowy, glittering peaks and ridges. At last, late in the afternoon, three great big-horn suddenly sprang up to our right and crossed the table-land in front of and below us at a strong, stretching gallop. The lengthening sunbeams glinted on their mighty horns; their great supple brown bodies were thrown out in bold relief against the white landscape; as they plowed with long strides through

26

the powdery snow, their hoofs tossed it up in masses of white spray. On the left of the plateau was a ridge, and as they went up this I twice fired at the leading ram, my bullets striking under him. On the summit he stopped and stood for a moment looking back three hundred and fifty yards off,* and my third shot went fairly through his lungs. He ran over the hill as if unharmed, but lay down a couple of hundred yards on, and was dead when we reached him.

It was after nightfall when we got back to the horses, and we rode home by moonlight. To gallop in such weather insures freezing; so the ponies shambled along at a single-foot trot, their dark bodies white with hoar-frost, and the long icicles hanging from their lips. The cold had increased steadily; the spirit thermometer at the ranch showed 26° Fahrenheit below zero. We had worked all day without food or rest, and were very tired. On the ride home I got benumbed before I knew it and froze my face, one foot, and both knees. Even my companion, who had a great-coat, froze his nose and cheeks. Never was a sight more welcome than the gleam of the fire-lit ranch windows to us that night. But the great ram's head was a trophy that paid for all.

* Actual pacing, not guesswork.

A MONTANA COWBOY.

THE GAME OF THE HIGH PEAKS:
THE WHITE GOAT

THE PONY OF THE NORTHERN ROCKIES.

XII

The Game of the High Peaks: The White Goat

IN the fall of 1886 I went far west to the Rockies
and took a fortnight's hunting trip among the
northern spurs of the Cœur d'Alêne, between
the towns of Heron and Horseplains in Montana. There are many kinds of game to be
found in the least known or still untrodden
parts of this wooded mountain wilderness—
caribou, elk, ungainly moose with great
shovel horns, cougars, and bears. But I
did not have time to go deeply into the
heart of the forest-clad ranges, and devoted
my entire energies to the chase of but one
animal, the white antelope-goat, then the
least known and rarest of all American game.

We started from one of those most dismal and forlorn of all places, a
dead mining town, on the line of the Northern Pacific Railroad. My foreman, Merrifield, was with me, and for guide I took a tall, lithe, happy-
go-lucky mountaineer, who, like so many of the restless frontier race, was
born in Missouri. Our outfit was simple, as we carried only blankets, a
light wagon sheet, the ever-present camera, flour, bacon, salt, sugar, and
coffee: canned goods are very unhandy to pack about on horseback. Our
rifles and ammunition, with the few cooking-utensils and a book or two,
completed the list. Four solemn ponies and a ridiculous little mule named
Walla Walla bore us and our belongings. The Missourian was an expert
packer, versed in the mysteries of the "diamond hitch," the only arrangement of the ropes that will insure a load staying in its place. Driving a
pack train through the wooded paths and up the mountain passes that we

had to traverse is hard work anyhow, as there are sure to be accidents happening to the animals all the time, while their packs receive rough treatment from jutting rocks and overhanging branches, or from the half-fallen tree-trunks under which the animals wriggle; and if the loads are continually coming loose, or slipping so as to gall the horses' backs and make them sore, the labor and anxiety are increased tenfold.

In a day or two we were in the heart of the vast wooded wilderness. A broad, lonely river ran through its midst, cleaving asunder the mountain chains. Range after range, peak upon peak, the mountains towered on every side, the lower timbered to the top, the higher with bare crests of gray crags, or else hooded with fields of shining snow. The deep valleys lay half in darkness, hemmed in by steep, timbered slopes and straight rock walls. The torrents, broken into glittering foam masses, sprang down through the chasms that they had rent in the sides of the high hills, lingered in black pools under the shadows of the scarred cliffs, and reaching the rank, tree-choked valleys, gathered into rapid streams of clear brown water, that drenched the drooping limbs of the tangled alders. Over the whole land lay like a shroud the mighty growth of the unbroken evergreen forest—spruce and hemlock, fir, balsam, tamarack, and lofty pine.

Yet even these vast wastes of shadowy woodland were once penetrated by members of that adventurous and now fast vanishing folk, the American frontiersmen. Once or twice, while walking silently over the spongy moss beneath the somber archways of the pines, we saw on a tree-trunk a dim, faint ax-scar, the bark almost grown over it, showing where, many years before, some fur-trapper had chopped a deeper blaze than usual in making out a "spotted line"—man's first highway in the primeval forest; or on some hill-side we would come to the more recent, but already half-obliterated, traces of a miner's handiwork. The trapper and the miner were the pioneers of the mountains, as the hunter and the cowboy have been the pioneers of the plains; they are all of the same type, these sinewy men of the border, fearless and self-reliant, who are ever driven restlessly onward through the wilderness by the half-formed desires that make their eyes haggard and eager. There is no plain so lonely that their feet have not trodden it; no mountain so far off that their eyes have not scanned its grandeur.

We took nearly a week in going to our hunting-grounds and out from them again. This was tedious work, for the pace was slow, and it was accompanied with some real labor. In places the mountain paths were very steep and the ponies could with difficulty scramble along them;

IN A CAÑON OF THE CŒUR D'ALÊNE.

and once or twice they got falls that no animals less tough could have survived, Walla Walla being the unfortunate that suffered most. Often, moreover, we would come to a windfall, where the fallen trees lay heaped

crosswise on one another in the wildest confusion, and a road had to be
cleared by ax work.   It was marvelous to see the philosophy with which
the wise little beasts behaved, picking their way gingerly through these
rough spots, hopping over fallen tree-trunks, or stepping between them
in places where an Eastern horse would have snapped a leg short off,
and walking composedly along narrow ledges with steep precipices

DOWN BRAKES !

below. They were tame and friendly, being turned loose at night, and
not only staying near by, but also
allowing themselves to be caught
without difficulty in the morning;
industriously gleaning the scant
food to be found in the burnt places
or along the edges of the brooks,
and often in the evening standing
in a patient, solemn semicircle
round the camp fire, just beyond
where we were seated. Walla
Walla, the little mule, was always
in scrapes. Once we spent a morning of awkward industry in washing our clothes; having finished,
we spread the half-cleansed array
upon the bushes and departed on a hunt. On returning, to our horror
we spied the miserable Walla Walla shamefacedly shambling off from
the neighborhood of the wash, having partly chewed up every individual
garment and completely undone all our morning's labor.

At first we did not have good weather. The Indians, of whom we
met a small band,—said to be Flatheads or their kin, on a visit from the
coast region,—had set fire to the woods not far away, and the smoke
became so dense as to hurt our eyes, to hide the sun at midday, and to
veil all objects from our sight as completely as if there had been a heavy
fog.   Then we had two days of incessant rain, which rendered our camp
none too comfortable; but when this cleared we found that it had put
out the fire and settled all the smoke, leaving a brilliant sky overhead.

We first camped in a narrow valley, surrounded by mountains so tall
that except at noonday it lay in the shadow; and it was only when we
were out late on the higher foot-hills that we saw the sun sink in a flame
behind the distant ranges.   The trees grew tall and thick, the underbrush
choking the ground between their trunks, and their branches interlacing

so that the sun's rays hardly came through them.   There were very few open glades, and these were not more than a dozen rods or so across. Even on the mountains it was only when we got up very high indeed, or when we struck an occasional bare spur, or shoulder, that we could get a glimpse into the open.   Elsewhere we could never see a hundred yards ahead of us, and like all plainsmen or mountaineers we at times felt smothered under the trees, and longed to be where we could look out far and wide on every side; we felt as if our heads were in hoods.   A broad brook whirled and eddied past our camp, and a little below us was caught in a deep, narrow gorge, where the strangling rocks churned its swift current into spray and foam, and changed its murmurous humming and splashing into an angry roar.   Strange little water wrens—the water-ousel of the books—made this brook their home.   They were shaped like thrushes, and sometimes warbled sweetly, yet they lived right in the torrent, not only flitting along the banks and wading in the edges, but plunging boldly into midstream, and half walking, half flying along the bottom, deep under water, and perching on the slippery, spray-covered rocks of the waterfall or skimming over and through the rapids even more often than they ran along the margins of the deep, black pools.

White-tail deer were plentiful, and we kept our camp abundantly supplied with venison, varying it with all the grouse that we wanted, and with quantities of fresh trout.   But I myself spent most of my time after the quarry I had come to get—the white goat.

White goats have been known to hunters ever since Lewis and Clarke crossed the continent, but they have always ranked as the very rarest and most difficult to get of all American game.   This reputation they owe to the nature of their haunts, rather than to their own wariness, for they have been so little disturbed that they are less shy than either deer or sheep.   They are found here and there on the highest, most inaccessible mountain peaks down even to Arizona and New Mexico; but being fitted for cold climates, they are extremely scarce everywhere south of Montana and northern Idaho and the great majority even of the most experienced hunters have hardly so much as heard of their existence.   In Washington Territory, northern Idaho, and north-western Montana they are not uncommon, and are plentiful in parts of the mountain ranges of British America and Alaska.   Their preference for the highest peaks is due mainly to their dislike of warmth, and in the north—even south of the Canadian line—they are found much lower down the mountains than is the case farther south.   They are very conspicuous animals, with their snow-white coats and polished black horns, but their pursuit necessitates so much toil and hardship that not one in ten of the professional hunters has ever killed one; and I know of but one or two Eastern sportsmen who can boast a goat's head as a trophy. But this will soon cease to be the case; for the Canadian Pacific Railway has opened the haunts where the goats are most plentiful, and any moderately adventurous and hardy rifleman can be sure of getting one by taking a little time, and that, too, whether he is a skilled hunter or not, since at present the game is not difficult to approach. The white goat will be common long after the elk has vanished, and it has already outlasted the buffalo. Few sportsmen henceforth—indeed, hardly any—will ever boast a buffalo head of their own killing; but the number of riflemen who can place to their credit the prized white fleeces and jet-black horns will steadily increase.

The Missourian, during his career as a Rocky Mountain hunter, had killed five white goats. The first he had shot near Canyon City, Colorado, and never having heard of any such animal before had concluded afterward that it was one of a flock of recently imported Angora goats, and accordingly, to avoid trouble, buried it where it lay; and it was not until fourteen years later, when he came up to the Cœur d'Alêne and shot another, that he became aware of what he had killed. He described them as being bold, pugnacious animals, not easily startled, and extremely tenacious of life. Once he had set a large hound at one which he came across while descending an ice-swollen river in early spring. The goat made no attempt to flee or to avoid the hound, but coolly awaited its approach and killed it with one wicked thrust of the horns; for the latter are as sharp as needles, and are used for stabbing, not butting. Another time he caught a goat in a bear trap set on a game trail. Its leg was broken, and he had to pack it out on pony-back, a two-days' journey, to the settlement; yet in spite of such rough treatment it lived a week after it got there, when, unfortunately, the wounded leg mortified. It fought most determinedly, but soon became reconciled to captivity, eating with avidity all the grass it was given, recognizing its keeper, and grunting whenever he brought it food or started to walk away before it had had all it wished. The goats he had shot lived in ground where the walking was tiresome to the last degree, and where it was almost impossible not to make a good deal of noise; and nothing but their boldness and curiosity enabled him ever to kill any. One he shot while waiting at a pass for deer. The goat, an old male, came up, and fairly refused to leave the spot, walking round in the underbrush and finally mounting a great fallen log, where he staid snorting and stamping angrily until the Missourian lost patience and killed him.

For three or four days I hunted steadily and without success, and it was as hard work as any that I had ever undertaken.   Both Merrifield and I were accustomed to a life in the saddle, and although we had varied it with an occasional long walk after deer or sheep, yet we were utterly unable to

THE INDIANS WE MET.

cope with the Missourian when it came to mountaineering.   When we had previously hunted, in the Big Horn Mountains, we had found stout moccasins most comfortable, and extremely useful for still-hunting through the great woods and among the open glades; but the multitudinous sharp rocks and sheer, cliff-like slopes of the Cœur d'Alêne rendered our moccasins absolutely useless, for the first day's tramp bruised our feet till they were sore and slit our foot-gear into ribbons, besides tearing our clothes. Merrifield was then crippled, having nothing else but his cowboy boots; fortunately, I had taken in addition a pair of shoes with soles thickly studded with nails.

We would start immediately after breakfast each morning, carrying a light lunch in our pockets, and go straight up the mountain sides for hours at a time, varying it by skirting the broad, terrace-like ledges, or by clambering along the cliff crests. The climbing was very hard. The slope was so steep that it was like going upstairs; now through loose earth, then through a shingle of pebbles or sand, then over rough rocks, and again over a layer of pine needles as smooth and slippery as glass, while brittle, dry sticks that snapped at a touch, and loose stones that rattled down if so much as brushed, strewed the ground everywhere, the climber stumbling and falling over them and finding it almost absolutely impossible to proceed without noise, unless at a rate of progress too slow to admit of getting anywhere. Often, too, we would encounter dense underbrush, perhaps a thicket of little burnt balsams, as prickly and brittle as so much coral; or else a heavy growth of laurel, all the branches point-ing downward, and to be gotten through only by main force. Over all grew the vast evergreen forest, except where an occasional cliff jutted out, or where there were great land-slides, each perhaps half a mile long and a couple of hundred yards across, covered with loose slates or granite bowlders.

We always went above the domain of the deer, and indeed saw few evidences of life. Once or twice we came to the round foot-prints of cou-gars, which are said to be great enemies of the goats, but we never caught a glimpse of the sly beasts themselves. Another time I shot a sable from a spruce, up which the little fox-headed animal had rushed with the agility of a squirrel. There were plenty of old tracks of bear and elk, but no new ones; and occasionally we saw the foot-marks of the great timber wolf.

But the trails at which we looked with the most absorbed interest were those that showed the large, round hoof-marks of the white goats. They had worn deep paths to certain clay licks in the slides, which they must have visited often in the early spring, for the trails were little traveled when we were in the mountains during September. These clay licks were mere holes in the banks, and were in spring-time visited by other animals besides goats; there were old deer trails to them. The clay seemed to contain something that both birds and beasts were fond of, for I frequently saw flocks of cross-bills light in the licks and stay there for many minutes at a time, scratching the smooth surface with their little claws and bills. The goat trails led away in every direction from the licks, but usually went up-hill, zigzagging or in a straight line, and continually growing fainter as they went farther off, where the animals scattered to their feeding-grounds. In the spring-time the goats are clad with a dense coat of long white wool, and there were shreds and tufts of this on all the twigs of the bushes under which the paths passed; in the early fall the coat is shorter and less handsome.

Although these game paths were so deeply worn, they yet showed very little fresh goat sign; in fact, we came across the recent trails of but two of the animals we were after. One of these we came quite close to, but never saw it, for we must have frightened it by the noise we made; it certainly, to judge by its tracks, which we followed for a long time, took itself straight out of the country. The other I finally got, after some heart-breaking work and a complicated series of faults committed and misfortunes endured.

I had been, as usual, walking and clambering over the mountains all day long, and in mid-afternoon reached a great slide, with half-way across it a tree. Under this I sat down to rest, my back to the trunk, and had been there but a few minutes when my companion, the Missourian, suddenly whispered to me that a goat was coming down the slide at its edge, near the woods. I was in a most uncomfortable position for a shot. Twisting my head round, I could see the goat waddling down-hill, looking just like a handsome tame billy, especially when at times he stood upon a stone to glance around, with all four feet close together. I cautiously tried to shift my position, and at once dislodged some pebbles, at the sound of which the goat sprang promptly up on the bank, his whole mien changing into one of alert, alarmed curiosity. He was less than a hundred yards off, so I risked a shot, all cramped and twisted though I was. But my bullet went low; I only broke his left fore-leg, and he disappeared over the bank like a flash. We raced and scrambled after him, and the Missourian, an excellent tracker, took up the bloody trail. It went along the hill-side for nearly a mile, and then turned straight up the mountain, the Missourian leading with his long, free gait, while I toiled after him at a dogged trot. The trail went up the sharpest and steepest places, skirting the cliffs and precipices. At one spot I nearly came to grief for good and all, for in running along a shelving ledge, covered with loose slates, one of these slipped as I stepped on it, throwing me clear over the brink. However, I caught in a pine top, bounced down through it, and brought up in a balsam with my rifle all right, and myself unhurt except for the shaking. I scrambled up at once and raced on after my companion, whose limbs and wind seemed alike incapable of giving out. This work lasted for a couple of hours.

The trail came into a regular game path and grew fresher, the goat having stopped to roll and wallow in the dust now and then. Suddenly, on the top of the mountain, we came upon him close up to us. He had just risen from rolling and stood behind a huge fallen log, his back barely

showing above it as he turned his head to look at us.   I was completely
winded, and had lost my strength as well as my breath, while great bead-
like drops of sweat stood in my eyes; but I steadied myself as well as I
could and aimed to break the backbone, the only shot open to me, and not
a difficult one at such a short distance.   However, my bullet went just too

THE FIRST SHOT.

high, cutting the skin above the long spinal bones over the shoulders; and
the speed with which that three-legged goat went down the precipitous
side of the mountain would have done credit to an antelope on the level.

Weary and disgusted, we again took up the trail.   It led straight
down-hill, and we followed it at a smart pace.   Down and down it went,
into the valley and straight to the edge of the stream, but half a mile above
camp. The goat had crossed the water on a fallen tree-trunk, and we took
the same path.   Once across, it had again gone right up the mountain.
We followed it as fast as we could, although pretty nearly done out, until
it was too dark to see the blood stains any longer, and then returned to
camp, dispirited and so tired that we could hardly drag ourselves along,
for we had been going at speed for five hours, up and down the roughest
and steepest ground.

But we were confident that the goat would not travel far with such a wound after he had been chased as we had chased him.   Next morning at daybreak we again climbed the mountain and took up the trail.   Soon it led into others and we lost it, but we kept up the hunt nevertheless for hour after hour, making continually wider and wider circles.   At last, about midday, our perseverance was rewarded, for coming silently out on a great bare cliff shoulder, I spied the goat lying on a ledge below me and some seventy yards off.   This time I shot true, and he rose only to fall back dead; and a minute afterward we were standing over him, handling the glossy black horns and admiring the snow-white coat.

After this we struck our tent and shifted camp some thirty miles to a wide valley through whose pine-clad bottom flowed a river, hurrying on to the Pacific between unending forests.   On one hand the valley was hemmed in by an unbroken line of frowning cliffs, and on the other by chains of lofty mountains in whose sides the ravines cut deep gashes.

The clear weather had grown colder.   At night the frost skimmed with thin ice the edges of the ponds and small lakes that at long intervals dotted the vast reaches of woodland.   But we were very comfortable, and hardly needed our furs, for as evening fell we kindled huge fires, to give us both light and warmth; and even in very cold weather a man can sleep out comfortably enough with no bedding if he lights two fires and gets in between them, or finds a sheltered nook or corner across the front of which a single great blaze can be made.   The long walks and our work as cragsmen hardened our thews, and made us eat and sleep as even our life on the ranch could hardly do: the mountaineer must always be more sinewy than the horseman.   The clear, cold water of the swift streams too was a welcome change from the tepid and muddy currents of the rivers of the plains; and we heartily enjoyed the baths, a plunge into one of the icy pools making us gasp for breath and causing the blood to tingle in our veins with the shock.

Our tent was pitched in a little glade, which was but a few yards across, and carpeted thickly with the red kinnikinic berries, in their season beloved of bears, and from the leaves of which bush the Indians make a substitute for tobacco.   Little three-toed woodpeckers with yellow crests scrambled about over the trees near by, while the great log-cocks hammered and rattled on the tall dead trunks.   Jays that were dark blue all over came familiarly round camp in company with the ever-present moose-birds or whisky jacks.   There were many grouse in the woods, of three kinds,—blue, spruce, and ruffed,—and these varied our diet and also furnished us with some sport with our rifles, as we always shot them in rivalry.   That is, each would take a shot in turn, aiming at the head of the bird, as it perched motionless on the limb of a tree or stopped for a second while running along the ground; then if he missed or hit the bird anywhere but in the head, the other scored one and took the shot.   The resulting tally was a good test of comparative skill; and rivalry always tends to keep a man's shooting up to the mark.

Once or twice, when we had slain deer, we watched by the carcasses, hoping that they would attract a bear, or perhaps one of the huge timber wolves whose mournful, sinister howling we heard each night.   But there were no bears in the valley; and the wolves, those cruel, crafty beasts, were far too cunning to come to the bait while we were there.   We saw nothing but crowds of ravens, whose hoarse barking and croaking filled the air as they circled around overhead, lighted in the trees, or quarreled over the carcass.   Yet although we saw no game it was very pleasant to sit out, on the still evenings, among the tall pines or on the edge of a great gorge, until the afterglow of the sunset was dispelled by the beams of the frosty moon.   Now and again the hush would be suddenly broken by the long howling of a wolf, that echoed and rang under the hollow woods and through the deep chasms until they resounded again, while it made our hearts bound and the blood leap in our veins.   Then there would be silence once more, broken only by the rush of the river and the low moaning and creaking of the pines; or the strange calling of the owls might be answered by the far-off, unearthly laughter of a loon, its voice carried through the stillness a marvelous distance from the little lake on which it was swimming.

One day, after much toilsome and in places almost dangerous work, we climbed to the very top of the nearest mountain chain, and from it looked out over a limitless, billowy field of snow-capped ranges.   Up above the timber line were snow-grouse and huge, hoary-white woodchucks, but no trace of the game we were after; for, rather to our surprise, the few goat signs that we saw were in the timber.   I did not catch another glimpse of the animals themselves until my holiday was almost over and we were preparing to break camp.   Then I saw two.   I had spent a most laborious day on the mountain as usual, following the goat paths, which were well-trodden trails leading up the most inaccessible places; certainly the white goats are marvelous climbers, doing it all by main strength and perfect command over their muscles, for they are heavy, clumsy seeming animals, the reverse of graceful, and utterly without any look of light agility.   As usual, towards evening I was pretty well tired out, for it would be difficult to imagine harder work than to clamber unendingly up and down the huge cliffs. I came down along a great jutting spur, broken by a series of precipices, with flat terraces at their feet, the terraces being covered with trees and bushes, and running, with many breaks and interruptions, parallel to each other across the face of the

STALKING GOATS.

mountains. On one of these terraces was a space of hard clay ground beaten perfectly bare of vegetation by the hoofs of the goats, and, in the middle, a hole, two or three feet in width, that was evidently in the spring used as a lick. Most of the tracks were old, but there was one trail coming diagonally down the side of the mountain on which there were two or three that were very fresh. It was getting late, so I did not stay long, but continued the descent. The terrace on which the lick was situated lay but a few hundred yards above the valley, and then came a level, marshy plain a quarter of a mile broad, between the base of the mountain and the woods. Leading down to this plain was another old goat-trail,

28

which went to a small, boggy pool, which the goats must certainly have often visited in the spring; but it was then unused.

When I reached the farther side of the plain and was about entering the woods, I turned to look over the mountain once more, and my eye was

THE WHITE GOAT AT HOME.

immediately caught by two white objects which were moving along the terrace, about half a mile to one side of the lick. That they were goats was evident at a glance, their white bodies contrasting sharply with the green vegetation. They came along very rapidly, giving me no time to get back over the plain, and stopped for a short time at the lick, right in sight from where I was, although too far off for me to tell anything about their size. I think they smelt my footprints in the soil; at any rate they were very watchful, one of them always jumping up on a rock or fallen log to mount guard when the other halted to browse. The sun had just set; it was impossible to advance across the open plain, which they scanned at every glance; and to skirt it and climb up any other place than the pass down which I had come — itself a goat-trail — would have taken till long after nightfall. All that I could do was to stay where I was and watch them, until in the dark I slipped off unobserved and made the best of my way to camp, resolved to hunt them up on the morrow.

Shortly after noon next day we were at the terrace, having approached with the greatest caution, and only after a minute examination, with the field-glasses, of all the neighboring mountain. I wore moccasins, so as to make no noise. We soon found that one of the trails was evidently regularly traveled, probably every evening, and we determined to lie in wait by it, so as either to catch the animals as they came down to feed, or else to mark them if they got out on some open spot on the terraces where they could be stalked. As an ambush we chose a ledge in the cliff below a terrace, with, in front, a breastwork of the natural rock some five feet high. It was perhaps fifty yards from the trail. I hid myself on this ledge, having arranged on the rock breastwork a few pine branches through which to fire, and waited, hour after hour, continually scanning the mountain carefully with the glasses. There was very little life. Occasionally a chickaree or chipmunk scurried out from among the trunks of the great pines to pick up the cones which he had previously bitten off from the upper branches; a noisy Clarke's crow clung for some time in the top of a hemlock; and occasionally flocks of cross-bill went by, with swift undulating flight and low calls. From time to time I peeped cautiously over the pine branches on the breastwork; and the last time I did this I suddenly saw two goats, that had come noiselessly down, standing motionless directly opposite to me, their suspicions evidently aroused by something. I gently shoved the rifle over one of the boughs; the largest goat turned its head sharply round to look, as it stood quartering to me, and the bullet went fairly through the lungs. Both animals promptly ran off along the terrace, and I raced after them in my moccasins, skirting the edge of the cliff, where there were no trees or bushes. As I made no noise and could run very swiftly on the bare cliff edge, I succeeded in coming out into the first little glade, or break, in the terrace at the same time that the goats did. The first to come out of the bushes was the big one I had shot at, an old she, as it turned out; while the other, a yearling ram, followed. The big one turned to look at me as she mounted a fallen tree that lay across a chasm-like rent in the terrace; the light red frothy blood covered her muzzle, and I paid no further heed to her as she slowly walked along the log, but bent my attention towards the yearling, which was galloping and scrambling up an almost perpendicular path that led across the face of the cliff above. Holding my rifle just over it, I fired, breaking the neck of the goat, and it rolled down some fifty or sixty yards, almost to where I stood. I then went after the old goat, which had lain down ; as I approached she feebly tried to rise and show fight, but her strength was spent, her blood had ebbed away, and she fell back lifeless in the effort. They were both good specimens, the old one being unusually large, with fine horns. White goats are squat, heavy beasts ; not so tall as black-tail deer, but weighing more.

Early next morning I came back with my two men to where the goats were lying, taking along the camera. Having taken their photographs and skinned them we went back to camp, hunted up the ponies and mules, who had been shifting for themselves during the past few days, packed up our tent, trophies, and other belongings, and set off for the settlements, well pleased with our trip.

All mountain game yields noble sport, because of the nerve, daring, and physical hardihood implied in its successful pursuit. The chase of the white goat involves extraordinary toil and some slight danger on account of the extreme roughness and inaccessibility of its haunts ; but the beast itself is less shy than the mountain sheep. How the chase of either compares in difficulty with that of the various Old World mountain game it would be hard to say. Men who have tried both say that, though there is not in Europe the chance to try the adventurous, wandering life of the wilderness so beloved by the American hunter, yet when it comes to comparing the actual chase of the game of the two worlds, it needs greater skill, both as cragsman and still-hunter, to kill ibex and chamois in the Alps or Pyrenees—by fair stalking I mean ; for if they are driven to the guns, as is sometimes done, the sport is of a very inferior kind, not rising above the methods of killing white-tail in the Eastern States, or of driving deer in Scotland. I myself have had no experience of Old World mountaineering, beyond two perfectly conventional trips up the Matterhorn and Jungfrau—on the latter, by the way, I saw three chamois a long way off.

My brother has done a good deal of ibex, mountain sheep, and markoor shooting in Cashmere and Thibet, and I suppose the sport to be had among the tremendous mountain masses of the Himalayas must stand above all other kinds of hill shooting ; yet, after all, it is hard to believe that it can yield much more pleasure than that felt by the American hunter when he follows the lordly elk and the grizzly among the timbered slopes of the Rockies, or the big-horn and the white-fleeced, jet-horned antelope-goat over their towering and barren peaks.

Adios.